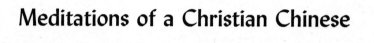

Meditations of a Christian Chinese

Meditations

of a

Christian Chinese

by REV. DR. Y. T. CHIU, Ph.D.

Chao Ên-tz'ŭ

Associate Professor of Chemistry, Huntington College, Huntington, Indiana, Pastor of the Heap Gay and Zion Churches in Hong Kong and British Territory

PAGEANT PRESS -:- NEW YORK

Published by Pageant Press, Inc.
130 West 42nd Street, New York 36, New York

First Edition
LIBRARY OF CONGRESS CATALOG CARD NUMBER: 56-13118

Manufactured in the United States of America

1020582

Dedicated

to

my Parents

MR. AND MRS. C. C. CHIU

CONTENTS

Preface

Since I have written twenty-four books and over ninety tracts in Chinese, many of my English-speaking friends have asked me to write a book in English for them to read.

Some of the chapters of this book are translations from those which appeared in my books printed in Chinese, while several are topics of my speaking engagements. They will give the reader an idea of some of my scientific and Christian experience as well as my philosophy of life.

I sincerely hope that this book will give the reader facts about China and the Christian service rendered by Chinese Christians for the extension of God's kingdom.

"There is a great and growing interest in China and your Table of Contents led me to feel that you have a book that should be well received in this country," wrote Mr. Seth Richards, publisher of the Pageant Press, in his letter. The author sincerely hopes that this book will present the conditions of China today and he humbly asks all readers to remember China in prayers that things will come out in accordance with God's will.

Finally, I want to express my appreciation and thanks to my friend and colleague, Professor William John Thomas, Jr., for his kindness in reading several chapters of this book and for his friendly advice and criticisms. I also wish to thank Dr. Elmer Becker, president of Huntington College, and all members of the faculty of Huntington College, Rev. Edmund C. Burkey, pastor of the College Park U.B. Church, Huntington, Indiana, Mrs. F. A. Loew, Miss Effie Hodgeboom, Rev. Ernest Gingerich and many other friends for their criticisms and encouragement.

This book is dedicated to my parents, Mr. and Mrs. C. C. Chiu, to whom I am indebted for my Christian education and training and for their many prayers for me during their lifetime.

Y. T. Chiu

May 10, 1956

The Value of the Sunday School in China

Many Christians in China do not see the real value of having a Sunday school and ask themselves these questions: (1) Why do we have to attend Sunday school? (2) What benefit do we get from it? (3) Is it worthwhile to go to Sunday school? Some think that the Sunday school is good for smaller children only and many young students refrain from going because they do not see the purpose of the Sunday school.

Personally, I believe that the Sunday school is the best place for moral and spiritual development. Let me relate my personal experience. When I was six years old, my father took me to the Baptist Sunday school in Hong Kong. Having formed the habit of going to the Sunday school, my attendance was quite regular. When I was a freshman at the University of California, I became a Sunday school teacher at a Chinese mission school in Berkeley, California. I have taught Sunday schools in China for more than thirty years. When illness has prevented my attendance, it has been a source of deep regret for me.

The Sunday school lessons have been very helpful to me through these years, and my memory has been strengthened by memorizing the golden texts, which have been valuable to me. Not until I began teaching a Sunday school class did I realize the value of the lessons which I have received. Needless to say, I did not appreciate the Sunday school at first, and the only reasons I attended were because of my mother's wishes and to receive a picture card every Sunday. I soon found that the stories in connection with each lesson were interesting, and they contained moral lessons which strengthened my character. Through these lessons many of my life problems were solved. I greatly appreciated my Sunday school teachers who were very kind and helpful to me. Many of the most valuable friendships of my life were formed through such associations.

I now realize that it is the duty of every Christian to attend Sunday school and to help in any way he can. In this way we learn more about God and are encouraged to become better Christians and to render service to the church, to society and to the world. Pupils should co-operate with the teacher in trying to make the Sunday school attractive and interesting. Some lessons may seem uninteresting; nevertheless, they contain the right kind of food for the soul.

In China, the church and Christian schools cannot get along without the Sunday school. As we do not have compulsory religious education in schools, all Christian training must be accomplished through the Sunday school and Bible classes. The students in China need a spiritual awakening. Therefore the church must avail itself of this splendid opportunity for deepening the spiritual channel by getting the younger generation to join the organization which places emphasis upon spiritual values.

The Sunday school prepares young men and women to become members of the church. The best Christians are those who have been thus prepared for Christian service and from among these will come the future leaders of the church. Realizing this value, all Christian schools have been encouraging their non-Christian students to attend the Sunday schools. Through the influence of the Sunday school teachers, many students have been baptized and brought into church membership. At the end of the year, rewards are given to those who have the best record of attendance. Each child in attendance receives a Bible picture card and this helps keep the attendance regular. Shall we pray for the work of the Sunday school in China?

Our Rural Christian Work

BEFORE RENDERING CHRISTIAN SERVICE TO THE VILLAGE PEO-
ple, we made inspection trips to study the village life and conditions of the people in the country. It was found that ninety
percent of these poor village people are illiterate and most of
them are very poor. In the smaller villages there are no schools
for their children. Schools are only found in larger villages and
nearly all of these schools are much below the standard.

The sanitary conditions in these villages are very bad. The
streets are very narrow, muddy and dirty. One can find pigs,
chickens, dogs, ducks and geese which make the streets very dirty.
Many of the houses were built with mud bricks dried under the
sun. These houses are very small, but each house is fully occupied.
They are dark, poorly ventilated and dirty. In these houses idols
are given their prominent places. Although the poor villagers
cannot afford to send their children to schools, they waste a great
deal of their money in buying incense and sacrifices for their
gods. The average farmer would spend much money for a wedding feast. They have to borrow money for the expenses of their
wedding and the new couple has to work hard the rest of their
lives in order to pay off their debts due to their marriage.

We found that the death rate is very high among village children. This is due to the unsanitary conditions of their homes and
the ignorance of the mothers who do not know how to take care

of their children. Smallpox, cholera, dysentery, typhoid, tuberculosis and venereal diseases are quite common in these villages, and they do not know the cause of these diseases or the methods for their prevention. Most of them do not want to go to the hospital when they are sick. Patients would only go to the hospital when they are dying. This accounts for the fact that the majority of the sick people who go to the hospital are hopeless and go there "to die." This is why they are afraid to go to the hospital for treatment. It was found that the village mothers do not know how to feed their babies. Many of them feed their babies with rice or rice cakes from birth. The average mother had from eight to ten children, but only two or three of these children live to reach manhood.

This gives us the background for our Christian work among the poor village people.

We have founded free schools in many villages. We found that it was more difficult to teach these village children since they had dirty habits. They used bad language. Our teachers said that these children were taught to steal, to tell lies, to swear, to cheat and to fight by their older relatives before they came to our schools. One day one child said to his teacher who taught him to brush his teeth every morning: "My parents never brush their teeth, why should I?" Other children have a hard time to break away from evil customs and bad habits.

We have organized missionary bands going out to these villages every Sunday afternoon. We gave them free vaccination and medical care.

In the villages there is not a single church where the people can go. Our Zion Church in Kowloon, opposite Hong Kong, has been rendering good Christian services. Miss W. C. Kwan, our registered nurse, is greatly respected, because she has rendered valuable service to the people living in the vicinity of our Zion Church for more than fifteen years. Rev. S. Y. Wong, pastor of our Zion Church, and his family live in one of the nearby villages.

Our Bible women preach the Gospel to these villagers and teach them not only to give up idol worship and gambling, etc. They also teach them to be pure and honest. We must show them the Christian way of life and lead them to see that hatred, jealousy, evil thoughts, cheating, telling lies and swearing will injure the soul.

We carry on our evangelical work from village to village. Each Sunday our Bible women bring children to the Sunday school and quite a few of the adults go to our church services.

We find that there is no duplication of our rural work as the work of churches is centered in towns and cities. Since most of the people in South China live in villages, the problem of working among the rural districts is quite important. The poorer farmers must be given an opportunity to hear the gospel of Christ. They need medical care and attention. They are hungry both physically and spiritually. Their children should have an opportunity to go to school. Child labor should be eliminated. They need some one to show them the Christian way of life. We are anxious that more souls be saved and many be won to Christ.

3

The Prodigal Son's Brother

(Luke 15:25-32)

IN OUR READING OF THE SCRIPTURE, WE OFTEN PAY ATTENTION to the prodigal son and do not consider his brother. In this story our Lord wants to emphasize, in the character of the prodigal son, that repentance is absolutely necessary no matter how much sin a man has, and that our heavenly Father always feels happy whenever a sinner repents of his sin and is willing to go back to Him and ask for His forgiveness.

As to the prodigal son's brother who thinks that he is a good man and need not repent, we know that such a character is not approved by Jesus. He is not welcomed in the kingdom of God. Let us examine his character carefully.

In the first place, the prodigal son's brother lacks love. His father loves him just as much as his brother. He is so happy in his father's home where he has everything he wants that he is not conscious of his privileges and advantages. He has no love for his brother. He knows that his brother is a sinner and a prodigal son, but has he done anything to help him? When his bad brother got lost, did he try his best to look for him and to save him? His brother is a sinner. He considers him to be dead forever and is no longer his brother. Therefore he has no love for him. If a man does not love his own brother (no matter how bad he is), how can he love his enemy as Jesus has taught us to love our enemies? John says we cannot love God, if we do not love our own brother. We must remember that a brother is a brother no matter whether he is good or bad. So this prodigal son's brother is wrong when he loves his brother only when he behaves himself, but feels indifferent to him and does nothing for him when he is bad.

In the second place, we find that the prodigal son's brother is jealous of his brother's good treatment. He does not understand why his bad brother is treated so well when he returns home. He thought his bad brother ought to be severely punished when he came back. The trouble with him is that he is jealous of other people who, he thinks, receive better treatment than he. It is easier for a man to rejoice when other people are not as good as he is. But we must learn to be happy when other people become happy, to "rejoice with the angels when sinners repent and return to God." A man feels happy when he loses a very expensive diamond ring and finds it again after a long search for it. He is happy because he loves his valuable ring. Should not one be happier when his lost brother returns home, a brother who is dead because of his sins and is saved? The prodigal son's brother may not be as bad as his brother, but God would not consider him to be good if he is jealous of others and is not satisfied with his own splendid opportunities and possessions.

Thirdly, the prodigal son's brother is too selfish. He can only think of his own pleasure, his own comfort, and his own good environment. He has no sympathy for those who suffer. He does not care whether people are hungry or suffer because of their sins. He feels indifferent when his own brother is starving, because he wasted and spent all his father's money. He thought his brother deserved physical punishment because of his own sins. If he were a Christian, he could not have felt happy when his own brother became a servant of Satan. His duty was to go at once to save his brother. If he does nothing for others when

9

other people are suffering from their sins, he is selfish. God is not pleased with a selfish man.

Fourthly, the prodigal son's brother is too lazy. When his brother got lost he was too lazy to go to do something for him. Yes, he is busy with his own work, but knowing that his brother has gone wrong and that he has done nothing for him, he is a lazy person. If a mother who sees her sick child and does nothing for him is considered lazy, so the prodigal son's brother is lazy because he does not want to take the trouble to do something to rescue his own brother. A Christian is lazy when he does nothing for God to save others from sin. A man is not considered to be good when he only attends to his own work and does nothing to help others. No one should be lazy in this world when so many people have been ruined by Satan. There is plenty of work for him to do in order that others may hear the gospel and be saved by Jesus. If we should follow the bad example of the prodigal son's brother, we would be just as lazy as he is.

Fifthly, this prodigal son's brother is self-righteous. He thinks he is a good man and has no sin and therefore need not repent. His brother is bad because he has sinned. But he is not as good as his brother because he does not know his own sin. John says a man who knows what is right and does not do right is a sinner. A man who does not love his own brother is also a sinner. Now this man who considered himself to be good and righteous and does nothing to help other people is also a sinner. His brother knows his own sins and is willing to repent, but he feels he needs no repentance, therefore he cannot be welcomed in the kingdom of God.

In this world there are many people who are like the prodigal son's brother. Christians feel cool and indifferent when they know that countless numbers of people who are our brothers and sisters have sinned against God and they do nothing to help them. God's will cannot be done unless we, as Christians, try our best to co-operate with God in the war against sin and evil, and to save our brothers from the devil. And when people are saved and turned back to God, we ought to rejoice with the angels in heaven.

4

My Testimony

I WANT TO THANK GOD FOR THE WONDERFUL WORK OF JESUS Christ in my life. I was very selfish and proud when I was a boy. When going to school with my younger brother, I would run away from him lest my friends knew that he was my brother. Born of Christian parents and being the grandson of the first Baptist minister in China (on my mother's side), I thought too much of myself. I had many ambitions, desiring to be rich and educated, before Christ got hold of me. I had to give up all my selfish ideas and learn to share my very best with other people.

I was jealous of others. When I found that friends were more brilliant or did better work than I, I was very jealous of them. I was awarded four first prizes from 1905 to 1908 while a student in Hong Kong. When I went to Berkeley, California, in 1908 to further my study, I found that some students were smarter than I. Sometimes I could not sleep at night because of jealousy. One evening, Jesus taught me a lesson. I was unhappy and could not study in my room, so I went for a walk. Shortly, I met a robber who pointed a pistol at me and searched my pockets. Fortunately, I had only one dollar in my pocket. I was so frightened that I said to myself, "Last night I had two hundred dollars in my pocket when I returned to my room from San Francisco. Had I been held up last night, I would not be able to pay my college expenses for one semester." I learned a lesson.

I knew that being jealous of other people was wrong. From that day on, I felt happy when other people were better off than I.

I once thought that since I did not gamble, or smoke, or drink alcoholic beverages, I would be a good Christian. But God wanted me to see that one is a sinner if he is selfish, jealous and impure. Christ has helped me to get rid of these evil habits. He is my Savior. He has saved me from the little sins which made me unhappy. Christ gradually changed my character from self-centered to one that is God-centered.

Many incidents in my life show God's protection and care. While a student at the University of California at Berkeley, I encountered a mad horse which was out of control. One of the iron shoes of the horse loosened and was thrown towards me. Fortunately the shoe did not strike me, but it broke a large window glass three feet away. While walking alone one day in Berkeley, I was almost killed by a train. In 1913, I went to Estes Park, Colorado, in training as a Y.M.C.A. secretary. One afternoon I went with several friends up the Rocky Mountains ten thousand feet above sea level. They climbed the mountain so fast that I could not follow them. About six o'clock in the evening I lost my way. It was getting dark and I was left alone. I did not know what to do. I knew that if I could not find my way I would be devoured by wild beasts. I cried to God and prayed to Him in great earnest. In one hour of frightful experience, thanks be to God, I was able to find my way and came to a small hotel. This happened 43 years ago and I still remember what God has done for me. His love and care can never be forgotten as long as I live. When in America for the second time in 1925, I escaped from two motor car accidents without the slightest injury. Although I lost my nerve in the accidents, I learned from them that God takes care of me. Praise be His holy name!

While in America from 1908 to 1915 studying for my B.S.

and M.A. degrees I had the opportunity of attending fourteen summer conferences for Christian students. I feel that I learned more that has been vital in my life and career at these Christian conferences than in the several years I spent at college. There I met many of the best Christian leaders and received a great deal of inspiration from them. It was in one of these conferences that I decided to give my life to Christ. I used to care more for material things, but Christ helped me sacrifice all I had for Him. I had to give up all my own ambitions, and my love for the things of this world—riches, reputation, honor, pleasures, etc., and sacrifice all I had and surrender myself to Christ. I had to learn to love the things that Christ loves and do the work that He wants me to do.

My religious life has been helped by my close connection with the Sunday school and church ever since I was a boy. In Berkeley, California, I taught Sunday school classes in two Chinese missions. During my college days I had the opportunity to preach in the Chinese churches in Oakland, San Francisco, Fresno, Sacramento and New York. I was so much interested in Christian service that when I got my B.S. degree in 1913 I spent one year as a Y.M.C.A. secretary, working among Chinese students along the Pacific coast, before I studied for my M.A. degree at Columbia University in 1914. This association with men of strong Christian character and rich experience has been very helpful to me. The joy of Christian service I had in those days can never be forgotten. The satisfaction of having done something for Christ cannot be compared with anything in this world.

I returned to China in 1915. Two years before, I was advised by a friend, Mr. T. Y. Lum, to devote my life to teaching. It was two years before I could make this decision, but with God's help I have remained a teacher and a preacher for over forty years. I have been tempted to give up teaching and to go either

14

into government service or into business where I could make
more money. My father did not want me to teach because a
teacher does not receive a large salary. But God made it clear to
me that, as a teacher, I would have greater opportunities to
render Christian service, and I would be happier in the end. I
have had to learn to be patient and satisfied even with a smaller
income. I realize that in the kingdom of God, the value of
Christian service and that of Christian character count more
than material gain or wealth. Thus, I learned the lesson of laying
up treasure in heaven.

At Lingnan University, besides devoting my time to teaching
chemistry and mathematics, I had splendid opportunities to do
Christian service on the campus and outside as well. For five
years I was asked to help in the financial campaigns of the
Y.M.C.A. in Canton. I won the championship in 1928. I was
elected as a director of the Y.M.C.A. Besides this I served on
the Boards of ten Christian schools. Many Christian schools asked
me to speak to the students on Science and Christianity and
preach at their Sunday services. I have been leader of Bible
classes and treasurer of more than twelve Christian organizations.
I was once treasurer of the True Light high school and college
auditor for many years. I am very grateful to Christ for having
given me these splendid opportunities for Christian service which,
in addition to the joy I get, strengthen my Christian character.

I enjoy singing in the choir, thus helping the Sunday service.
Christian service requires a great deal of time, but one who loves
Christ will never regret this. The only way to get rid of doing
evil is to get busy with Christian service. We work for Christ,
not because we want any reward or praise for our work, but
because it is our duty as a Christian. We want to do our very
best for Christ.

Great help has been given me during the last forty years by
my good wife who has great interest in my work. She sees my

15

weaknesses and points out my mistakes so that with God's help I can make improvement. She also sets a great example to me by spending a great deal of her time in prayer and in Bible study. Her interest in work for poorer people has inspired me to do more for them. I admire her for her unselfishness, her deep love for Christ, and her willingness to do all she can to further God's kingdom. As a result of her work I became interested in the Christian education of poorer children. Her methods of work are often better than mine. Thus with her co-operation we are able to do better work for the Master.

I often see my mistakes and my shortcomings. I may not have done my best for Christ, but I am willing to obey Him and do His will. Here is a summary of my Christian experiences of which I am only too glad to give my testimony. When I draw near to Christ and do what He wants me to do, I always feel happy. When I get away from Him, I am discouraged. God does answer prayer. In my very difficult times, in the days when no one can help me, Christ does help me. His love and His kindness and mercy shown to me and to my family cannot be described with words. So in my testimony, I do want to tell others of God's goodness, His love and help. He will help all those who love Him and will bless those who are faithful in Christian service. I sincerely hope that those who read my testimony may be inspired to do more work for our Lord. As He has helped me in the last forty-five years, He will certainly help and bless any one who will follow and serve Him.

What Christians Should Do in Time of Trouble

As Christians we should have the right attitude of mind in order to be able to do something in the midst of difficulties and uncertainties. We must be calm when we are in trouble. A nervous person cannot do anything to help others who are excited and nervous. As Christians we should read Psalm 118 thoughtfully and get lots of inspiration. Here we find the psalmist in the midst of great difficulties and danger. He was surrounded by enemies and in danger of losing his own life, but he did not lose his courage. He had perfect confidence in God, believing that "He is good and His mercy endureth forever. . . . It is better to trust in the Lord than to put confidence in man. . . . The Lord is my strength and song, and is my salvation. . . . The voice of rejoicing and salvation is in the tabernacles of the righteous: the right hand of the Lord doeth valiantly."

So a Christian who has perfect faith in God should be optimistic. We must not look solely at the present situation. We must look above and beyond where we can see better and much more. We have to hope for the best and only think of the best. When Peter left the ship and walked on the water to go to Jesus, and when he saw the wind was boisterous, he was afraid, and beginning to sink, he cried out saying, "Lord, save me," and immediately Jesus stretched forth His hand, and caught him,

17

and said unto him, "O thou of little faith, wherefore didst thou doubt?" (Matthew 14:29-31.) We would, like Peter, lose our courage and become pessimistic if we sat down, did nothing but read newspapers and listened to rumors and exaggerated reports and had all sorts of improper imaginations. We would be discouraged and broken-hearted, just as Peter was when he looked downward instead of upward. Let us look above the dark clouds and beyond the boisterous waves to our Lord for help and guidance, and He will stretch forth His hand to help and save us from harm. God is our rock and shelter, so why should we be discouraged or pessimistic?

A story is told of a ship going through dangerous waters. The passengers were very much excited. One of them ran up to see the captain. He found him standing on the bridge, looking calm and showing no signs of being anxious or nervous. The man went back to tell the other passengers they need not be afraid because the captain had not lost courage and was calm and cheerful. Jesus is our Captain. If we have a glimpse of Him, we shall find that He is quite calm and cheerful.

By looking at the world situation one might think that God is sleeping and does not mind what is going on in this world. But He is still living. He is still our Lord and cares for His children just as a father would care for his own children. He is doing wonderful work in this world which we cannot see. So we should have perfect confidence in Him.

There are some concrete things that we should do. First, we must remember that God answers prayers. So we should spend much time in prayer. We should pray for all persons who have been suffering. Above all, we should pray for permanent peace, international brotherliness and good will. Wonderful things can come out of prayer so that in days of peril or distress, we should not neglect our duty to pray.

Secondly, we find that many people do not have the courage

and confidence in God as we do. So we should try our best to encourage them. Our relatives and friends may come to us for advice. We must not make things worse by exaggerating or giving discouraging reports or helping to spread rumors. We should make things as pleasant and smooth as they can be, and encourage others to think deeply and guide them in their work and conduct. By being cheerful ourselves first, we can make others cheerful, happy and hopeful.

Thirdly, we should sacrifice some of our luxurious things and comforts, and give away things that we can spare in order to do something to help those who are in need. Nothing should be wasted and every effort made to save all we can so that we can help those who are less fortunate than we are.

Fourthly, we should in no way let our work be interrupted. It is very difficult to carry on our work when we are in distress. If we concentrate our minds on our work, we shall find that nothing can bother us. A mother who is used to hearing her child cry will not give up her work simply because her child cries. We have to adjust ourselves in such a way that we can do our work as usual and work as hard as we can, just as if nothing would happen. It is not easy at first, but we can train ourselves so that nothing will bother or interfere with our work.

Fifthly, we should do all we can to enlarge our Christian activities. Remember that God is with us and He is ready to help us. He expects us to do more for Him.

Lastly, we must co-operate with God in His great task of setting things right, in His plan of salvation and in His fight against sin, selfishness, jealousy, covetousness, unrighteousness, pride, hatred, prejudice and misunderstanding—all these things which bring about war and suffering in this world.

How An Overseas Chinese
Regained His Christian Faith

THIS IS AN INTERESTING STORY OF A CHINESE BUSINESS MAN who spent about twenty years in Boston, Massachusetts, where he made his fortune. His name is Mr. M. T. Chan and his native village is Toy San where most of the Chinese who own laundries and Chinese restaurants in the United States come from.

Mr. Chan was baptized in a church in Boston in 1912. He was a nominal Christian. He saved a lot of money and returned to Canton, China, in 1927 to spend the rest of his life with his family. He built a house in the west part of Canton, where most of the rich people stay. He was having the best comforts he could get in life. So everyone who knew him thought that he must be a very happy man. Although he was a Christian, he did not act like a good Christian. He did not use part of his money to do good, such as helping the poor, supporting orphans, etc. In other words, he had been a miser. He was so careful with his money that he did not deposit it in the banks in Canton, fearing they would go into bankruptcy. So he put his money under his pillow every night when he went to bed. One day a robber learned about his great wealth and decided to steal his money. A snake was brought into his house. He was so frightened that he ran out of his house, but forgot to take his money with him. So he was robbed of a great sum of money.

Having lost much of his fortune and realizing that it would not be safe to stay in Canton, he sold his house and built a smaller one in Hato village near Lingnan University, one of the thirteen Christian colleges in China. His house was the largest one, however, in the village. Shortly after he and his family moved to Hato village, his house was burned down and the only thing he could take out of his house was his Bible. What bad luck had happened to poor Mr. Chan!

The Chinese proverb says that "blessings would seldom come doubled, while misfortunes never come single-handed." Mr. Chan had four sons and several daughters. Like other people from the Toy San village, he was very fond of boys. However, he lost three of his four sons. The eldest son was drowned while swimming. His other two sons died of sickness. They were buried side by side in a Christian cemetery in Canton. Mr. Chan became a Chinese Job. Having lost his fortune and three sons, Mr. Chan almost lost his Christian faith, which is much more valuable. We cannot blame him for being disappointed and pessimistic.

One day while my wife and a Bible woman were conducting an evangelical meeting in the Hato village, she was told of Mr. Chan's bad luck. My wife went to see him and had a long talk with him. He seemed to be a little encouraged. She asked him to come to attend her evangelical meetings. He got interested and repented of his sins. He became a better Christian and felt much happier. So Mr. Chan was saved by Jesus Christ. He was born again. He came to our church quite regularly with his family. He and his wife joined one of our missionary bands. They went from village to village to preach the Gospel. His hairs were all gray and he looked old, but he became a happier man because, although he had lost his earthly riches and his three sons, he had regained spiritual wealth from the Lord Jesus, which is the real blessing of life. Shortly after the end of World War II, Mr. Chan passed to his eternal reward, while his wife and children went to Hong Kong as refugees.

21

Child Welfare in China

Many parents in China do not know how to take care of their children, so they either have bad habits or have their health ruined. Some people think that the care and teaching of children should be left entirely to teachers in schools. In South China the well-to-do mothers leave their children entirely in the hands of maid-servants. Poorer people who are unable to employ servants have so many children to take care of that their older children have to help their mothers take care of their baby brothers or sisters, who are carried on their backs all day long. Sometimes one can see in the slums in Canton and Hong Kong children carrying a small baby brother or sister on their backs and playing on the streets or helping their parents do some sort of household work at the same time. Some women who are rowing a boat or pulling a heavy wagon are seen carrying babies on their backs. In the rich families, infants are carried on the backs of maid-servants. Only very few mothers who have a good education know how to take care of their own children, otherwise they would be "spoiled" quite easily.

Many mothers seem to like boys better than girls. In some rural districts girls are seldom welcomed in their homes. Sometimes boys receive better treatment, better food and clothing, etc., than their sisters in the same home. Some old folks (grandmothers, aunts, etc.) are so fond of boys that they let them have their own way and would not have them punished or reproved when they do wrong. Some stubborn old folks would not allow their girls to receive a higher education. In the Christian homes, this is quite different. Through the influence of Christianity, boys and girls receive equal treatment and are given the same opportunity for education and training.

In Lingnan University before the war, twenty per cent of the students were girls. The True Light high school and the Pooi To high school for girls founded by American missionaries in the suburbs of Canton consist of three hundred and six hundred girl students respectively. So Christianity has a good influence in changing the Chinese homes so that parents pay better attention to their children. Sixty years ago many girls were forced to have their feet bound. This evil custom has been eradicated. In large cities the majority of the girls prefer to have their hair bobbed. Thirty years ago very few Chinese young women would go to a beauty parlor. It is quite different now, as one finds these young ladies patronizing the beauty parlors. This shows how fast western culture and civilization are welcomed in China.

Very few mothers know how to feed their babies. If the infant were fed with mother's milk, it would be better for the child. But we often find that the poorer people feed their babies with "chewed" rice or rice cakes shortly after birth. As cow's milk is so expensive in South China, very few mothers can afford to buy cow's milk for their children. The writer has analyzed several kinds of milk substitutes made locally and sold in the stores in Canton and found that they consist of starch and a little sugar (less than one-half of one per cent of this substituted milk is protein). In North China soya bean milk is used in feeding babies. This is much cheaper than cow's milk. This bean milk is made by soaking soya beans overnight in water so that they become soft and easy to grind in a stone mill. Water is added while the beans are being ground and the milk is filtered through cloth bags. One pound of soya beans would make seven or eight pounds of bean milk. As soya bean milk is deficient in fat, sugar and calcium, the latter should be added to the bean milk to increase its food value. Dr. Siddall used this milk to feed a baby in the Canton hospital and got pretty good results. If soya bean milk is prepared in a sanitary condition, it should be a good and cheap food for poorer babies.

One cause of infant mortality, which is very high in China, is the unsanitary conditions in the homes. Only the well-educated mothers know that fresh air, sunshine and nourishing food are essential to the health of their babies. Many homes are very dark, dirty and very poorly ventilated. Babies are either underfed or overfed. Milk bottles are not sterilized so that babies who survive are the ones who have the highest resistance to germs of disease. Furthermore, hundreds of children die from infectious diseases each year.

Clothing for babies is very simple. Many of them are re-modeled from the old ones of older children or of adults. Some think that it would be a waste of money to make new clothes for smaller children. Some mothers force their children to wear too many clothes lest they catch cold. Cotton is mostly used for making children garments. Red, which is a symbol for happiness, is chosen for children's garments on Chinese New Year, for a wedding ceremony and for festivals and special occasions. White clothes are used for mourning.

Many superstitious people do not call their children by their proper names and call them "pig" or "dog" or "shrimp" or "bull," etc., lest evil spirits should know them and do them harm. When the children get sick, they think that they are being troubled by evil spirits, so they go to the temple to pray to the gods or employ some Taoist or Buddhist priests to come to offer prayers for their sick children. Sometimes children wear certain kind of ornaments for their own safety. Jade is chosen as it is believed to balance the body and prevent the child from falling. When a child begins to go to school, he carries some celery which is a symbol for diligence. Some old people think that bean curd, a product made from soya beans, should not be given to infants lest they have an offensive odor on their breaths. Old eggs, especially ducks' eggs, are not to be eaten by boys lest they get deformities in their bodies. These customs vary with different places. In the Christian homes they are done away with. No Christian is allowed to worship his dead ancestor.

In an old-fashioned home, children are not allowed to talk or ask questions. A good child is considered to be quiet or inactive. If a child is disobedient, he is threatened by something to frighten him, so as to force him to obey.

The non-Christians are beginning to see the importance of nursery and kindergarten education. They know that if a child is not taught to do the right thing when he is very young, he may grow up to cause trouble to the community.

Chinese children like to play. In many homes in South China, they are not allowed to play lest they break some of the furniture or windows or do something to injure themselves. In an old school, a child is taught that "diligence would bring honor to the family while play is harmful." This shows that a child is not encouraged to play. Returned students have brought a change in the old system of education, so that many schools in Canton and Hong Kong have good playgrounds for children.

Many smaller children eat what the adults are eating. Some of the food is hard for them to digest. This is one of the causes of indigestion, etc. Poor diet has hindered the growth of many Chinese children. In Canton, hundreds of children die of smallpox, cholera, typhoid, dysentery, diphtheria, meningitis, etc., from infection every year.

For the welfare of Chinese children, child labor should be abolished. We need public schools for these less fortunate children, and for the orphans who lost their parents during the war. Many schools have boy scouts and girl scouts in South China. The Y.M.C.A. and Y.W.C.A. are rendering good Christian service to Chinese children today.

An Ancient Chinese Diplomat

ONCE UPON A TIME IN THE STATE OF CHI IN CHINA, THERE WAS a diplomat whose name was Yen. He was noted for his eloquence. He was sent by the king of Chi to the state of Cho. In order to test his intelligence, the king of Cho opened a small gate to welcome him.

Yen was not pleased with this impolite treatment and said to the king of Cho: "Your majesty made a mistake by opening a wrong gate to let me in. This small gate is the dog's hole, and is intended for one who wants to go to the state of dogs. I am not sent by my king to the state of dogs, therefore I cannot enter by this gate."

The king of Cho was silent and opened the large gate to welcome Yen and apologized for his "mistake." Then he invited Yen to his palace where all the ministers gathered in a hall to welcome the eloquent statesman from the state of Chi.

Then the king of Cho said to Yen: "Why did your king send you to my state? Are there no noblemen in your state?"

Yen replied: "There are, of course, many noblemen in my state, but my king has sent them all to other states."

Although the king felt that he was mocked, yet he could not answer a word.

Several days later, the king of Cho tried to take vengeance on Yen for his insult. So he invited him to a banquet. By previous arrangement a man was arrested and was brought before the king who asked: "Who is this man?"

They replied: "He is a man from the state of Chi."

"Why have you arrested him?" asked the king.

"He is a thief," they replied.

Then the king said to Yen: "Ah! Your people of the state of Chi make their living by stealing."

Yen did not lose his temper, but said gently to the king: "It is said that sweet oranges only grow on the south side of the Wei river where our state of Chi is located. But if these fruit trees are planted on the north side of the river, that is in the state of Cho, they would become thorns. How can sweet orange trees be changed into thorns? It is because of the difference in soil and climate. Well, the people of the state of Chi do not steal in their own state, but when they come to your state, they would become thieves. Is not this due to the difference in soil and climate too?"

The king knew that he had again been outwitted by Yen, so he could not say a word. He had to change his attitude toward Yen and treated him kindly and with respect.

This story shows that we should treat all foreigners or aliens with love and respect. Confucius said: "What you do not want done to yourself, do not do to others." This is the negative side of reciprocity. Christ gave us the positive side in His Golden Rule. He said: "Therefore all things whatsoever ye would that men should do to you, do ye even so to them; for this is the law and the prophets." (Matthew 7:12.) If we would eliminate racial prejudice, treat all foreigners or aliens with love and respect, and treat them as friends, we would cultivate international brotherliness and good will. We would do away with war and we would have permanent peace.

The king of Cho learned a good lesson and realized his mistake in ill-treating a famous statesman from his neighboring state. May this also be a lesson to those who show personal hatred and prejudice towards the aliens living in their own country.

Chinese Missionary Bands

MISSIONARY BANDS IN CHINA WERE ORGANIZED IN 1936 BY S. C. Sung, Ph.D., the famous Chinese evangelist who conducted evangelistic meetings for many years in China. Wherever Dr. Sung went, before the end of a series of revival meetings, he spoke to the congregation about the importance of preaching the gospel in order to fulfill the commandment of Jesus Christ, "Go ye into all the world to preach the gospel." He often quoted the words of St. Paul: "Woe is unto me, if I preach not the gospel!" (I Corinthians 9:16.) Many Christians have been inspired by these words and so wanted to join one of the preaching bands.

There were one hundred and twenty missionary bands in Canton and fifty in Hong Kong before the war. Each band consists of from three to seven persons (not more than seven are allowed in each band). Each band should have a captain or chairman, a vice-chairman or vice-captain and a secretary. In each city there should be one superintendent and two assistant superintendents.

The city of Canton is so large that it is divided into five sections, namely the eastern section, the southern section, the western section, the northern section and the middle section, each section consisting of twenty-five bands. They should meet once a week. All the missionary bands meet once a month for report and prayer.

Each member of the missionary bands should contribute at least ten cents each month for the expenses which consist mostly of printing tracts on evangelistic topics.

The work of our missionary bands is as follows: (1) To go out to the different villages and tell the people about Christ. (2) To visit the sick in all the hospitals in the city and talk to them about Christ, telling them how sin ruins the soul, as disease does harm to the human body. (3) To preach the Gospel to the soldiers who otherwise have no opportunity to know anything about Christ. Permission has to be obtained before members of our bands are admitted to the city prisons. Only those who have a genuine love of Christ and passion for souls, care to talk to prisoners about Christ. (4) To hold meetings, giving an opportunity to all who want to come. This phase of work is very important and is similar to that of the Salvation Army except that no musical instruments other than a small accordion or mouth organ are used, and our band members do not wear uniforms. (5) To visit the homes of those who are interested as well as those who have never heard anything of the Gospel. (6) To preach the Gospel to passengers in steamers, junks, boats and trains, giving them our tracts which tell them about the Christian salvation through our Lord Jesus Christ. Here are splendid opportunities to tell people about Christ. We must not let the sellers of patent medicine enjoy the privilege of talking to the passengers, but we should be as eager to advertise for Christ as these money-making people are to advertise their own goods. In other words, we can learn their method of presentation in order to make our preaching as interesting and as attractive as possible. (7) To preach the Gospel to the refugees.

Members of our missionary bands should spend much time each day in prayer and Bible study. We must pray before we go out to preach. Remember that preachers are seed-sowers sowing the seed of the Word of God. As the farmers who sow the seed have to depend on nature to do the rest, so we have to depend on God for His guidance and help. It is our duty to do what we are told—that is to preach the Gospel to all men. God will take care of the rest. May the missionary bands in China under the guidance of the Holy Spirit do good work for the salvation of souls and for the glory of God.

Chinese Bible Women

A BIBLE WOMAN IS ONE WHO IS EMPLOYED BY THE CHURCH TO assist the pastor in doing the work of the church. In Canton, Hong Kong and large cities in South China, most churches employ one pastor, one assistant or student pastor, one or more Bible women, one general or executive secretary and one or more janitors. The general secretary acts like a Y.M.C.A. secretary, attending to all business matters and doing all the clerical work of the church. These assist the pastor in doing Sunday school work, in conducting evangelistic, prayer and revival meetings, in special church services, such as Christmas, Easter, etc., and in visitation work. They also preach the gospel in various places and help in bringing people to the church.

In 1937, before the war, there were four schools in Canton for the training of Bible women; one of them was more than twenty years old. Formerly, training of Bible women was not considered important, so that the majority of them received no training at all. Some of them could hardly read or write Chinese. It was thought that any one who had zeal and enthusiasm for Christian work would be qualified.

For the last thirty-two years the mission in China of the United Brethren in Christ has selected as Bible women not only those women who have passions for souls, but those who have been well-trained and have experience in doing personal work.

The work of Bible women is as follows:

1. To preach the Gospel to the relatives of our students by

visiting their homes, giving them messages of salvation and telling them about Jesus Christ. They help distribute our tracts and books to those who can read Chinese. There is a splendid opportunity for the Bible women to do personal work in the homes, because our Bible women are,Sunday school and Bible teachers, and our students know them. They are welcomed in the homes since Chinese women respect teachers and welcome them as teachers rather than as preachers.

2. To bring people to church and Sunday school and revival meetings. They find out those who are interested and bring them to our church meetings.

3. To visit the sick and those who have misfortunes in the family.

4. To conduct Bible and Sunday school classes. We have Bible classes for church members, students and servants, and special ones for village people.

5. To do social work, such as reforming the homes, doing away with evil customs, superstition, etc. Mrs. K. Y. Tse convinced many women that idol worship is wrong so that they burned the idols and gave up gambling.

6. To help collect and distribute old clothes, mosquito nets, used shoes and give them to those in need. Miss W. C. Kwan, who has been a midwife for twenty years near our Zion Church in Kowloon, Hong Kong, said that many babies were born without any clothes prepared for them by their mothers because they are very poor. She has to make and give away little garments to these less fortunate infants.

7. To render Christian service to the refugees during the war and after the war. In other words, a Bible woman is a Christian worker, who is versed in the Bible and ready to give the messages of God's salvation, rendering valuable service to those in need both physically and spiritually. She helps to extend the kingdom of God by winning souls to Christ.

Chinese Evangelists and Their Work

Fᴏʀᴛʏ ʏᴇᴀʀs ᴀɢᴏ ᴄʜɪɴᴇsᴇ ᴇᴠᴀɴɢᴇʟɪsᴛs ᴡᴇʀᴇ ǫᴜɪᴛᴇ ʀᴀʀᴇ. Many churches in China had to wait for foreign missionaries to come to conduct revival meetings which were strictly evangelistic. Before the war, we were very fortunate to have some of the world's best Christian workers, like Dr. John R. Mott, Dr. Sherwood Eddy, Dr. Stanley Jones, etc., to speak to the Chinese youth on important Christian topics, such as Christ and Students, The Importance of Evangelizing China in This Generation, How to Make Jesus Christ Real, The Fight for Character, Temptations of Students, etc. When they came to Canton and Hong Kong, no church was large enough to accommodate a congregation of several thousand people. Special meetings had to be held in a Chinese theatre, while people who wanted to attend these meetings were admitted by tickets obtained in advance. At that time Chinese students were very anxious to learn something about Christianity. In Canton, Hong Kong and other large cities in China where these famous evangelists had visited and spoken, hundreds of Chinese students signed pledges to join Bible classes, while many others wanted to stand for Christ by joining the church.

The students in China were greatly benefited by the work of these strong Christian leaders from America. Unfortunately they could not stay very long in China. In all the places where they preached, men and women were needed to do follow-up work. Bible classes or discussion groups on life problems and so on had to be organized, and those who made up their mind to accept Christ as their Savior, had to be taken proper care of and recommended to the various churches.

Everywhere one would find that church members often got "cold" or "lukewarm." They needed someone who came from other places to give them words of encouragement and the stimulus to do more work for Christ. The churches in China realized this need, and prayed to God for native evangelists to do the work of spiritual awakening. God has answered their prayers. There are now quite a few good evangelists in China who have various spiritual gifts. I am going to give a brief account of a few outstanding Chinese evangelists who spoke in the churches in South China before the war.

The best known evangelist in China is S. C. Sung, Ph.D., who was known as the "Chinese John the Baptist." Dr. Sung, who obtained his Ph.D. in organic chemistry from the University of Ohio in 1927, was a member of the Sigma Xi. He had a vision that God wanted him to be an evangelist. So he went to New York to study theology and returned to China to preach the Gospel. At first he was offered a good position to teach chemistry in a famous college in Peking. He rejected this offer, feeling that God's work was more important. So he sacrificed all he had and gave his life to Christ.

He was such an inspiring preacher that he was better known in China as an evangelist than as a chemist. He would rather become poor that more souls might be saved. He was despised by his friends, but God gave him strength and courage. Wherever he went, he drew large crowds to hear him. His sermons were several hours in length, but people never got tired of hearing him. He was the first evangelist in China to organize missionary bands, and thousands of Christians had been inspired to join. He was considered by many Christians as "the best and most forceful evangelist in China." In 1936 he conducted a summer Bible training school in Amoy near his native place, which was attended by more than two thousand Christians from all parts of China (several of them had to travel hundreds of miles by foot because they were very poor). Certainly Dr. Sung had done much for the churches in China. He had several narrow escapes from death, for he went to the war areas to preach the Gospel. One day his train was bombed by enemy planes, but God protected him from harm. When conducting revival meetings in Amoy in May, 1938, the city was bombarded and fell into the hands of the enemy, but he was quite safe, showing that God was with him and took good care of him. He died before the end of World War II at the age of forty.

Another good evangelist who visited South China is Rev. Marcus Chen. Like Dr. Sung, he was a returned student from America. Rev. Chen has been a teacher and preacher for over forty years. He has written many books on Christian subjects. His children, who also received their education and training abroad, are good Christian workers. Rev. Chen is quite strong, and is doing good work wherever he goes.

Rev. C. K. Cheng, another good evangelist, is a self-made man. He was so poor that his father could not afford to send him to school. But he studied by himself. Later a foreign missionary taught him English. He is the first preacher in China who studied through a correspondence school in theology. For many years he worked as a teacher and preacher in Changsha and conducted revival meetings whenever he was asked to do so.

Other Chinese evangelists who have done good work in South China are Mr. M. T. Wang, Dr. Leland Wang, Rev. Timothy S. K. Chao, Rev. Dr. Andrew Gih, Rev. Y. M. Chia, Rev. Theodore Chau, etc. Mr. M. T. Wang, who is a very eloquent preacher, is the editor of a church magazine in Peking which has a large circulation in Chinese churches. Mr. Wang has preached in South China many times and people like him. Dr. Leland Wang has conducted revival meetings not only in China, but also in Singapore, Malaya, Indonesia, Europe and America. Dr. Andrew Gih, like Dr. Leland Wang, has done extensive evangelistic work among the overseas Chinese in Asia, America, Formosa and the Philippines. He organized Bible schools and orphanages, was editor of many magazines and broadcast many of his sermons. Both Dr. Wang and Dr. Gih speak English fluently and have had many speaking tours in North America. We are very thankful to God that China now has good evangelists who have been chosen by Christ to do His work.

When Dr. Billy Graham conducted evangelistic meetings in Hong Kong in the spring of 1956, more than fifty thousand people came to hear him, while over four thousand people decided to give their hearts to Christ. Certainly "the harvest truly is plenteous, but the laborers are few: Pray ye therefore the Lord of the harvest, that He will send forth laborers into His harvest" in China, Hong Kong, Formosa, Southeast Asia and all over the world where there are Chinese.

The Appeal of Christianity to China

ALMOST ONE HUNDRED AND FIFTY YEARS HAVE GONE BY SINCE Dr. Robert Morrison, the first Protestant missionary, came to China to preach the gospel to the Chinese. He toiled hard for many years before he found the first Chinese convert. This does not mean that the Chinese were stubborn and refused to accept the Christian message of salvation. It means that it is not easy to get things started and that everything has a small beginning, and once it is started, it is less difficult to keep it going. We know that Dr. Morrison had much patience as a pioneer missionary from England and that he did not give up a very difficult task, though it looked discouraging in the beginning.

Dr. Morrison had to learn the difficult Chinese language, and it was not easy for him to find a teacher in those days, as very few Chinese knew English. For several years he worked very hard in order to master the language. In seven years of hard work he put out the first Chinese-English dictionary and translated the Bible into Chinese. There was much misunderstanding about Christianity, and very few people were friendly to the Christians, who were persecuted and ill-treated. The Chinese officials opposed Christianity and threatened to imprison or killed the Chinese Christians. Missionaries were called the "foreign devils." In spite of these handicaps, the pioneer missionaries toiled hard until the seed grew and multiplied, so that today there are more than two million Christians in China.

The Appeal of Christianity to China

Dr. Morrison's first convert and the first preacher (Rev. Faat Leung), whose grave is on the campus of Lingnan University, Canton, China, were Cantonese. The writer's grandfather on his mother's side (Rev. Mei Wong)—who is also the grandfather of Mrs. Moy Ling, whose husband was the first Chinese to be ordained as elder of the Church of the United Brethren in Christ—was the first pastor of the Chinese Baptist Church. When he was saved in California there were only three thousand Christians in China. We are indebted to the foreign missionaries for having established churches, hospitals, schools and charity organizations to care for the aged, the orphans, the blind, the lepers, etc., all over China. Even those people who are not friendly to the Christians have realized that the best institutions of learning are the mission schools and Christian colleges and universities. Chinese officials and anti-Christians sent their children to these Christian schools. When asked why he sent his children to study at Lingnan University (formerly called Canton Christian College), a prominent Chinese official who bitterly opposed Christianity answered: "Lingnan is a good school, so I sent my children there to study, but I do not want them to become Christians there."

In spite of the sacrifice and hard work of the Christian workers and foreign missionaries, attempts have been made to eradicate Christianity, because some people thought that Christianity had something to do with imperialism, capitalism and aggression. This is why there was a Boxer uprising in 1900 and an anti-Christian movement in 1924. In spite of persecution and opposition, the church in China grew steadily. Shortly after the anti-Christian movement, most of the churches in China were united into one church, called the Church of Christ in China, in order to get rid of denominational differences which are hard for the Chinese to understand, and to make Christianity less confusing to the non-believers. Then came the five-year movement to double the church membership, which soon reached over one million. All these have been good for the Chinese church and helped strengthen the faith of the Christians and deepen their love and enthusiasm for service. For Paul said: "We know that all things work together for good to them that love God." (Romans 8:28.)

As a result of the anti-Christian movement, hate for Christianity came into the minds of some political leaders, so that a law was passed forbidding the teaching of Christianity in schools and compulsory attendance of students in Sunday schools and church services. Bible study was to be taken out of the school curricula. The result is that students of the last three decades lack Christian training.

One may ask why it is so difficult for the Chinese to accept Christ as their Savior. The reasons are: (1) Most people think that since Jesus is a Western religious leader (they do not know that He was born in Palestine, which is Asia Minor), it would be better for the Chinese to have Confucius (born 550 years before Christ) whose teachings have great influence in the thoughts and culture of the Chinese. (2) If the slogan is "Asia for the Asians," then since Jesus is an Asian, He should be appropriate for all Asians. As there are less than twenty-five million Christians in Asia, the origin of Christianity and the great religions of the world, it is unfortunate that only half of one percent of the Chinese are Christians. (3) The Chinese find it hard to give up polygamy, gambling, worship of dead ancestors, etc.

For the last sixty years, the Chinese have suffered famine, plague, infectious diseases, flood, war and other calamities. Through suffering and trial, the Chinese have learned spiritual lessons from God.

Today the churches in China are reaping the harvest from the seed sown by the pioneer missionaries. The war scattered the

Chinese Christians who fled to West China or to other places of safety, where people have never heard of Jesus Christ. There they had opportunities to witness for Christ. During the war, people learned to understand the love of God and saw the work of the devil. Many Christian workers told us that people are more ready to accept Jesus Christ as their Savior. Up to date, church attendance in China has greatly increased so that there are three or four times more people going to church today than several years ago.

Dr. S. Lautenschlager said that when he was a missionary in China, he was asked to preach to the soldiers. He preached to them on the meaning of the Cross. He asked them: "Do you know the meaning of the Cross?" They said: "Yes, we know something about the cross." "What cross?" asked Dr. Lautenschlager. "We know the Red Cross," was the reply. Then Dr. Lautenschlager explained to these Chinese soldiers that without Jesus dying on the Cross, there would be no Red Cross to save human lives. One soldier said, "I want Jesus to save me. I want His Cross." This shows that the war helped our preaching, and made people understand the need of Christian salvation. We must show them that Christ will solve all problems and He is the hope of China and of the world.

We sincerely hope and pray that China will answer the appeal of Christianity and if China is evangelized, twenty-five percent of the world problem of evangelization will be solved by co-operation with the Prince of Peace.

Chinese Home Life

Chinese home life is different in different parts of the country. In some homes in South China, most men have gone abroad to earn their living, while their wives stay home to look after their children. Most homes have no modern conveniences. They are rather small and crowded with too many persons living in them.

Chinese home life is seldom happy unless it is Christianized, since many Christians lay much emphasis on an ideal Christian home. It is not happy for the following reasons:

1. Many mothers who are well-to-do leave their babies to the care of amahs (or maid-servants) who do not know how to take care of them. This accounts for so much sickness and death among Chinese babies. Not only is the birth rate high, but the death rate is also very high. Poorer parents leave their babies to the care of the older sisters or brothers, or carry them on their backs and take care of them when they are working at the same time.

2. Many rich men have too many wives or concubines in the home. This accounts for hatred, jealousy and quarrels or fights in the Chinese home. Sometimes women commit suicide or murder because of hatred and jealousy. Polygamy should be abolished in order to eliminate unhappiness in the home.

3. In many Chinese homes, girls are despised. They do not have the same opportunities as their brothers. Favoritism is the

cause of much uneasiness in the home. The half-brothers or sisters cannot get along with one another, while step-children do not receive equal treatment with the other children in the family, just as happened to the children of Jacob in the Old Testament story.

4. Superstition robs the home of its happiness; members of the non-Christian families often consult fortune-tellers for everything they do. They cannot marry or bury their dead until they select a "good" day. They are not free to do anything they want lest they annoy their gods or have bad luck.

5. Many Chinese mothers are illiterate. They cannot read or write. Many of the richer mothers spend their time in gambling or playing Mah-Jong (Chinese game) or going to the theatre. This is the cause of the paleness and weakness among many of the women in China.

6. Ignorance of the principles of nutrition and hygiene or sanitation is the cause of the spread of many diseases in China. Many children die from malnutrition, beriberi, anemia, tuberculosis, etc. The mothers should be taught how to keep their homes clean and free from disease germs. Many children are born blind because of the sins of their parents.

7. In spite of the fact that there are fewer broken homes and divorces in China, there is much unhappiness in the home because of worry over financial embarrassment. Many parents have been killed during the war and their homes destroyed by bombs. Because of war, most people do not have enough to eat. They feel hungry all the time, while very few have adequate meals. It is rather hard to find good jobs and both parents have to work, while many parents cannot send their children to schools or even to see the doctor when they are sick. Free clinics or dispensaries for poorer, needy children are scarce in China.

8. In the Chinese home, too many people live together under one roof. The older folks like to live together with their

wives and children, as well as with their grandchildren and great-grandchildren and other relatives. There are too many dependents in one home so that it is very difficult for one man to take care of so many people in his large family. Most of the homes are poorly ventilated or exposed to sunlight so that many get sick and die.

9. As the home is rather dark or poorly lighted, it is bad for the eyes of the children who study at night; so they have poor eyesight or become near-sighted and have to wear spectacles. Many children do not sit up straight when they read because their tables or chairs are not the proper height for them.

10. Many homes have not welcomed Christ into them. Family altars are scarce in the Christian homes. For without Christian love in it, no home can be really happy. People have to learn the Christian way of life, so that the family learn to love and forgive one another. Let Christ be the Head of each Chinese home, and every one of the family circle will feel happy and the home will be a "sweet, sweet home" and Christian folks will live together happy, for "there is nothing like home" when the Spirit of Christ permeates and abides in our homes in China.

14

A Mother's Love

Nearly all Chinese mothers love their children. They are willing to sacrifice for them. They want them to grow up to be good citizens. They are happy if their children are filial, obedient and diligent.

It is hard for those who have too many children to take care of them. They will be glad to send them to school, if they can afford it or to free schools sponsored by Christian people or philanthropists.

Good mothers should not spoil their children by letting them have their own way. Christian mothers should teach them to pray and read the Bible.

Chinese children love stories. The author has published two Bible stories for children.

It is a blessing for a child to have a good mother. Her love is very precious. God shows His love by giving His children good mothers who are anxious to teach them.

It is a pity that not all men love their children. There are those who are so selfish that they want to get rid of their children. One Christian father complains that he has too many children. He does not remember that these are God's precious gifts and that it is his duty to take good care of them.

Many Christian mothers in our churches in China follow the good example of Samuel's mother by dedicating their children to God. Many want their children to have a good Christian education, and they are taught to love God and render Christian service when they grow up.

It is true that because of extreme poverty, some parents would sell their children or let them be adopted by those without children. Only ignorant parents would give away their daughters to become concubines of richer men, while the most foolish parents would let their daughters become prostitutes for their selfish gain.

Here is a story of a father who consulted his wife about selling one or more of their children to meet the needs of the family. This has been told by many Chinese preachers in the pulpit.

In Central China there was a very poor man who had five sons. One day he said to his wife: "We have no money to buy food. I cannot find any job to take care of the children. We shall all starve if we do not do something before long." "What do you want to do?" asked the wife. "We must sell one of our sons that we may not die from starvation," was the reply.

His wife said, "Whom do you want to sell? They are all so dear to me." They knew that they could not sell their eldest son, because according to Chinese custom, the eldest son was considered to be the best child of the family. The father wanted to sell the second son, but the mother said, "You must not sell him, because he looks so much like me, and none of our children resembles me like he does."

They then considered the third child. "Our third child is the brightest in the family, so that it is hard for us to get rid of him," said the mother. "How about the fourth son?" asked the father. "He is not so good to me, because he is so weak and delicate."

But the mother said, "Our fourth son is so feeble that he would die, if he is sold, for nobody knows how to take care of him; so by all means we must spare him."

Lastly they considered the fifth son. The mother said in tears,

46

"Our youngest boy is so cute and lovely that I must keep him. After all I do not see how we could get rid of any of our five sons. I would die myself rather than sell any one of our dear children."

If this woman who has five sons could not spare any one of her dear children, how hard it was for God to give us His only begotten Son, that we might be saved through His death on the Cross.

15

The Importance of Kindergarten Work in China

KINDERGARTEN WORK IN CHINA IS LESS THAN FIFTY YEARS old. It was started by missionaries and it was only thirty years ago that it became universal. According to our experience, a child will become a better student if he has spent two or three years in the nursery school and kindergarten.

Kindergarten improves the character and conduct of a child. It is very important to train a child when he is young, just like a bush which can be bent to any desired shape much easier when it is very small. A Chinese proverb says: "A child at the age of three will have the same temper or behavior when he will be eighty years old." In other words you can tell the behavior of one at the age of three and at the age of eighty later. Solomon said: "Train up a child in the way he should go; and when he is old, he will not depart from it." (Proverbs 22:6.) This means that we must begin the training and education of a child in the kindergarten.

Chinese kindergarten students love to hear good stories of which they never get tired. So, we can give them good stories from the Bible and make use of the Sunday school and chapel to teach them to love God and to love one another, to be sincere and honest, and to hate sin and evil. There are many good stories which the kindergarten teacher may use to tell the youngsters so that they can learn the moral lessons from them. They will learn to fight for character and live the Christian life when they grow up. The kindergarten has certainly done a lot for the child by making him a better citizen for the future and by preparing him as a better leader for his country and for the church of God.

The kindergarten of the United Brethren in Christ was founded in 1828. During the last twenty-eight years we have found that the parents never felt regretful that they have sent their children to our kindergarten. They have appreciated the good work we have done. One rich parent who was not a Christian gave us money to buy furniture and equipment, and said our kindergarten was one of the best in Hong Kong.

Many parents in China do not know how to handle their younger children. They are cross and naughty at home and have bad habits. They have no toys and no place to play. Here in our kindergarten we want to correct their bad habits and help them form good ones. By using good pictures and toys and using object lessons, we can get our kindergarten students interested in our teaching, so that their attendance is very regular and punctual, and they all enjoy singing our songs and playing games which are good for them. Certainly, there are many things that a child in our kindergarten can learn which will do him good.

Seeing the value of kindergarten instruction, non-Christian schools also follow the good example of the Christian schools by having kindergartens. In Canton, the Union Normal School, which is one of the Christian schools, has trained many kindergarten teachers, some of whom went to Hong Kong and other places to teach. Good kindergarten teachers are in great demand and some even went abroad to further their study and to visit the kindergartens in Europe and America. As our kindergarten was one of the best in Canton before the war, the U.B. in Christ kindergarten was awarded a certificate by the Commissioner of Education and many officials sent their children to study in our kindergarten.

16

Giving

Every Christian should learn the important lesson of giving. The words of our Lord should be borne in mind: "It is more blessed to give than to receive."

It is not easy for one to share his possessions with others unless he is taught to do so when very young. In the Sunday school there are wonderful opportunities for the students to learn to give all they can for the Cause and to help those who are in need.

It is not easy for one who does not have the spirit of Christ to give away what he has to share with those in need. The rich young ruler seemed to be a good man, but after he had an interview with Jesus, he went away in sorrow, because he would not sell all he had, to give to the poor in order to be a disciple of Jesus. He never had any experience of giving as he was a rich miser.

We know that all the believers in the first century had "all things common. And sold their possessions and goods, and parted them to all men, as every man had need." (Acts 2:44, 45.) This was not easy for the early Christians to do. But they learned their lessons of giving and tithing from the apostles. Can Christians today learn the lesson of giving from the apostles?

One may ask the question, "Why do we have to give and share our good things with those who have none?" Of course, if everybody in this world were rich and good and happy, there would be no need of giving. But after two world wars, the majority of the people in this world are very poor. They are suffering, because they are in need of food, clothes, medicine, education, etc. Can we not do something for them while millions of people are starving and dying? Can we send bread to feed the hungry souls?

Many children in China do not have sufficient food to eat, as food is so expensive after the war. Many Chinese children are undernourished in China and Korea. Can we give something to help these unfortunate children?

In order to be able to give, we must learn to save our money and our food. As much food has been wasted, children have to learn to save, by remembering these poorer and less fortunate children. In a famine in China, students living in the dormitories of Lingnan University decided to give away three eggs each morning for one semester in order to use the money to help the famine victims. One missionary invited some guests to his home for dinner where nothing was served and the money intended for a good dinner was given to the China Famine Relief Fund.

In China, after many years of war, millions of people are in desperate condition. In South China alone there are thousands of children who have lost their parents and homes. Many of them are suffering from malaria, tuberculosis, anemia, etc., because of the lack of proper food and medical care. Some of them have been crippled for life by bombs dropped from the air during the war. Realizing the dire needs of these unfortunate children, can we be more sympathetic and do something for them?

In the miracle of feeding the five thousand, a small boy was willing to give up his lunch that Jesus might use it to feed others. Chinese children have been taught by their older relatives that "selfish boys will have much pain in having their hair cut" so that they will share their food with other children. There was a Chinese boy named Kung who was given the first choice of

51

pears. He chose the smallest one for himself. When asked why he chose the smallest one, he said the larger ones should be reserved for his elder brothers and older folks. So a child should learn to share with others and to give his best to help the ones in need.

As God has given His best to us that we may have salvation through the death of His only Son, we must give our best to Him, just as Abraham was willing to sacrifice his son born in his old age. It is hoped that each child in a Christian home in China is taught to give his best—his time, his money, his talent, and his heart to Christ, that others may be helped by his giving and that he will receive blessings from God, the Giver of all good gifts.

17

Spiritual Medicine

(I Peter 2:24; James 5:16)

We all have bodies both physical and spiritual. When our physical bodies become sick we need the care of medical doctors; if our souls have sickness, we should have spiritual medical treatment.

In Romans 1:28-32, St. Paul tells of our spiritual diseases which consist of unrighteousness, fornication, evil desire, hatred, envy, wickedness, covetousness, maliciousness, murder, deceit, malignity, evil talk, lying, back-biting, godlessness, pride, disobedience, covenant-breaking, unmercifulness, etc.

Jesus showed us our spiritual diseases by saying, ". . . out of the hearts of men, proceed evil thoughts, adulteries, fornications, murders, thefts, covetousness, wickedness, deceit, lasciviousness, an evil eye, blasphemy, pride, foolishness. . . ." (Mark 7:21-22.) All spiritual patients should get rid of the spiritual germ of disease—SIN—in order to have speedy recovery.

Jesus Christ can cure all kinds of spiritual diseases. He is our spiritual physician and surgeon. He said in Mark 2:17, "They that are whole have no need of the physician, but they that are sick: I came not to call the righteous, but sinners to repentance." Jesus healed both the physical and spiritual diseases of men.

Peter said, "Who his own self bare our sins in his body on the tree, that we, being dead to sins, should live unto righteousness: by whose stripes ye were healed." (I Peter, 2:24.) This shows that Jesus, in healing the spiritual diseases of men, made a great sacrifice and died on the cross that men could be saved.

All spiritual patients should have perfect confidence in Jesus, the Savior and Redeemer, who is the only spiritual doctor. His advice and spiritual remedy should be carefully followed.

During the last few decades, wonderful discoveries have been made in modern medicine. New drugs such as penicillin, streptomycin, sulfa drugs, etc., which cure diseases, have been found. We were told that about three thousand years ago, Solomon discovered a spiritual remedy. He said: ". . . the tongue of the wise is health." (Proverbs 12:18.) There are many good remedies for sick souls given in the Bible and Christian literature which are beneficial to our souls. We should study these carefully.

Solomon also discovered another spiritual remedy in Proverbs 17:22. "A merry heart doeth good like a medicine: but a broken spirit drieth the bones." This means that our hearts must be pure and holy, free from sin and guilt. When our souls are free from sin, they are as healthy as our physical bodies are when they are free from disease germs.

Preventive medicine is a great blessing to men. We know that vaccination and inoculation against infectious diseases are important. We must be careful that Satan be driven out of our souls. ". . . Resist the devil, and he will flee from you." (James 4:7.) This is spiritual preventive medicine.

In His preaching, Jesus told men to forsake their sins and repent in order to get rid of their spiritual filthiness, just as a patient is advised by a physician to take a dose of cathartic to clean up his dirty bowels. So sinners should come to Jesus that their souls be purified by His precious blood shed for all men.

Jesus spoke as a spiritual surgeon when He said, "and if thy hand offend thee, cut it off: it is better for thee to enter into life maimed, than having two hands to go into hell, into the fire that never shall be quenched." (Mark 9:43.) This is spiritual surgery emphasized by Christ. We should cut off sources of temptation. A spiritual operation to remove anything that hinders the growth and development of our souls or that which is injurious to our spiritual life, is extremely essential.

There are spiritual parasites that are harmful to us. They are: hypocrisy, selfishness, heresy, false prophecy, etc. We should follow the advice of our spiritual physician, Jesus, who said, "Watch ye and pray, lest ye enter into temptation. The spirit truly is ready, but the flesh is weak." (Mark 14:38.) This precaution should be taken by all men who do not want to have spiritual diseases.

When one gets sick, he should immediately consult a doctor. He should not wait until he gets worse. Listen to the warning of Jeremiah when he said, "For thus saith the Lord, thy bruise is incurable, and thy wound is grievous. There is none to plead thy cause, that thou mayest be bound up: thou hast no healing medicines." (Jeremiah 30:12-13.) This is the hopeless or fatal condition of a stubborn spiritual patient.

We are thankful to God that He has remedies for all sick souls. "For I will restore health unto thee, and I will heal thee of thy wounds, saith the Lord." (Jeremiah 30:17.) We should not discard God's promise. He sent us His Son, Jesus Christ, to be our spiritual physician and surgeon who is willing to give us spiritual healing when we come to Him.

Finally, when a man gets sick he is unable to do any work. When he has spiritual sickness, he is unable to do any work for God. Remember, that any spiritual disease may lead to spiritual death. We must keep our souls strong and healthy. We should take great precautions that our souls be free from disease germs

—sin—that destroy the health of our souls. We must avail ourselves of the splendid opportunity of the spiritual healing of the
greatest physician and surgeon, Jesus Christ, who is kind and
merciful and will never turn down any patient who comes to
Him for help.

18

Feeding A Hungry World

In MATTHEW 14:13-21, MARK 6:32-44, LUKE 9:10-17 AND John 6:1-14 we are told that our Lord Jesus fed five thousand men, besides women and children, using only five loaves and two fishes and twelve baskets of the fragments were taken up. In Matthew 15:32-39 and Mark 8:1-9 it is related that He fed four thousand men besides women and children with seven loaves and a few fishes while seven baskets of fragments of food were collected.

Jesus fed the multitudes because they were hungry and He had compassion on them, and because they could not buy food in the desert.

Before feeding them with physical food, Jesus gave them spiritual food and medical treatment. "And he received them, and spake unto them of the kingdom of God and healed them that had need of healing." (Luke 9:11.) His disciples saw the physical need of the people and called the attention of their Master to these needs. He wanted to do first things first, giving them spiritual food and divine healing first and then physical food.

We have a hungry world today and the problem of feeding it is a difficult one. We know that two world wars have turned so many places into deserts by bombing that there is not enough land for farming while many of the farmers have been killed, making food much more expensive than before the war.

In Hong Kong and South China, where rice is the chief food, one could, before the war, buy sixty pounds of good rice for one U.S. dollar. Now the price of rice has gone up to six pounds for one U.S. dollar. Food is from five to ten times higher than before the war, while wages and salaries are not increased proportionally.

The increase in food prices is so great that the average family in China does not have enough to eat and many of them suffer malnutrition. Before the war in 1937, because fruits and vegetables were so cheap and easy to get, there was practically no scurvy in China. Now in additon to scurvy, there are many people in China who suffer from nutritional diseases such as anemia, beriberi, xerophthalmia or night blindness, rickets, etc., so that vitamin pills have to be given to the poorer people. As milk is so expensive in Hong Kong and China, children have to be contented with soya bean milk which has been used to feed babies in China for two thousand years. In South China many mothers are feeding their babies with rice or rice cakes so that many babies are undernourished and milk has to be given them by churches and the Salvation Army. In both China and Africa there is a milk fund in the mission of the Church of the United Brethren in Christ and other churches for feeding small children who suffer malnutrition.

When we were in "free" China during the war with Japan, 1943-1945, we did not have money to take care of our school. We found it very difficult to find enough food for our teachers and students and Christian workers. We experienced hunger and thirst. There were few days during the war when we could get a good meal. Then we evacuated Hong Kong and Macao and moved to places in the provinces of Kwang-tung, Kwang-si, Hunan and Kiangsi. When we returned to Canton safely from Nanchang we were able to receive our regular appropriations and we were grateful for the relief fund sent to us by the

Woman's Missionary Association which enabled us to do something to feed hungry souls both physically and spiritually.

Jesus wanted His disciples to do something to feed the hungry multitudes. They knew that these people who came to the desert to see and hear Jesus, perhaps a few miles from home, were hungry and it was getting dark. The disciples could not see how they could get so much food to feed so many people, the number of whom might be over ten thousand.

It is a pity that none of the disciples could do anything to help the hungry people, except Andrew, who told Jesus that a lad had five loaves and two fishes. "But," Andrew said, "what are they among so many?"

The boy had to give up his luncheon that others might be fed. He was not selfish, but willing to share with others and his mother allowed him to do it. This boy was willing to sacrifice for the benefit of others. He was happy to give his best to the Lord.

In this country people could give up their pennies used for chewing gum, candies, chocolate, ice cream, etc., and send them to the mission headquarters so that poorer people abroad may be fed and be saved and won to Christ in China, Africa, Central and South America, India, Japan, Indonesia, etc. We must live consecrated lives, and give money to foreign missions so that hungry souls may be properly fed.

When we give our best to the Lord, He can use our gifts and multiply them so that more people can receive the benefit from them. When we keep things for our own use only and do not give to others, we cannot receive the blessings from God. But if we sacrifice and share our belongings with others, God will abundantly bless us and use our money for the good of those who are in dire need.

In a year of famine in China, students of Lingnan University in Canton, where I taught for twenty-seven years (1915-1942), were willing to give up their breakfast for three months and sent the equivalent thereof in money to feed the famine victims. Some of the parents of these sufferers had to sell their children in order to have money to buy food. Because of poverty, ninety percent of the parents in China cannot afford to send their children to school and these youngsters must either stay home to work or work as servants in the homes of the rich or in the factories. One can find six-year-old cow boys sitting on the backs of water buffaloes on small Chinese farms, as there are no tractors or threshing machines. Everything on the farm has to be done by hand. Our returned missionaries tell us that a worker in China, Africa, Jamaica or Honduras earns from fifty cents, or less, to $1.75 U.S. a day. He could hardly have enough money to support his mother, his wife and his children and himself with this meager income.

One woman in Hong Kong, whose husband earned about $20 U.S. a month, attempted to commit suicide with her older son in her arms several years ago by jumping from the third story of a house, leaving her younger son aged two weeks to the care of her husband. The poor sick boy died immediately from fracture of the skull while the mother was critically injured. She was taken to the hospital and Dr. Allen Huang, whom I baptized in our Heap Gay Church in Hong Kong in 1952, gave her first aid. After several weeks in the hospital she recovered. She was tried for the murder of her son in the Supreme Court in Hong Kong. Her neighbors came to give testimony that this woman loved her husband and her children. But because of extreme poverty and because the older son was sick, she felt she had to commit suicide.

The jury found her innocent and she was acquitted. Quite a few people commit suicide in Hong Kong daily because they cannot solve their food and other problems.

People in the Orient do not have enough to eat. Poorer people in China and Hong Kong eat rice, soya beans, bean sprouts, bean curds and salt fish or green vegetables. The poorest people have only rice, sweet potatoes, which are cheaper than rice, and soya sauce made from soya beans. Can we do something here to help feed the poor and hungry souls in our mission fields?

Jesus wanted His disciples to co-operate with Him in feeding the multitude. He wanted them to make people sit down in groups of fifty or a hundred so that they could be easily counted and served. He wanted them to help distribute the food in an orderly manner so that everyone among the ten thousand people could have his share of the food which was multiplied by divine hands.

Being Himself a creator, Jesus could do this thing that no scientist can explain or duplicate. Jesus Christ, being the Son of God, did not have to obey the laws of science as every student in the chemistry or physics laboratory must do when he performs his experiments. With God, nothing is impossible. Jesus fed the multitude twice in His days when He was here on earth. Certainly He can help us feed a hungry world today if we as Christians are willing to bring our gifts to Him so that He can use them and multiply them many times.

When the multitude was fed Jesus told His disciples to "gather up the fragments that remain, that nothing be lost." (John 6:12.) Fragments may be gathered and used for the glory of God and the good of those in need. Our Lord Jesus does not want us to waste anything that is given us. He does not want us to waste our time, our money, our energy and effort, and our food. We must save our surplus that we do not need, save it so that we may send it to those in dire need in all mission fields. We can save our food too. Do not throw any food away. Those who eat too much and are overweight may have to reduce, for the sake of their health as well as for the good of others who are hungry and do not have enough to eat. We should cook just enough for our families, eat everything on our plates and have nothing to

61

throw away.

In China the richer folks and the shops always cook a little more so that they may give what is left on the table to beggars.

When we eat, let us eat enough and not overeat. Think of the poor hungry souls far away who are waiting for you to feed them. Remember that money in our pockets or deposited in the bank, if unused, will do no good, but given to the Lord will bring blessings to the giver and benefit to the poor. "It is more blessed to give than to receive."

We should give nourishing food rich in protein, carbohydrates, fats, minerals and vitamins to feed the hungry world. We should give pure spiritual food to feed the hungry souls, spiritual food which is free from contamination by modernism, heathenism, or things which are carnal and worldly.

Remember that the Lord Jesus had compassion on the multitude. He looks down to the hungry and sinful world today and wants us to do something to feed these multitudes. We sincerely hope that more people will quit smoking and drinking, etc., and use the money to feed hungry souls.

"Wherefore do ye spend money for that which is not bread? and your labor for that which satisfieth not? hearken diligently unto me, and eat ye that which is good, and let your soul delight itself in fatness." (Isaiah 55:2.)

If a lad could give up his lunch to Jesus that the multitudes might be fed, can not we give up something so that the hungry world may be fed, both physically and spiritually, that more souls living in darkness and sin may be saved?

19

How the Chinese Celebrate Christmas

Dr. ROBERT MORRISON'S MISSION TO CHINA IN 1807 AS THE first Protestant missionary resulted in only seven Chinese being won to Christ during the twenty-seven years of his ministry in China. Less than one percent of the Chinese today are Christians. The majority of them do not celebrate Christmas.

But all Christians and some of the non-Christians do celebrate Christmas. They have Christmas trees and Santa Claus whom they call "old man from the North Pole" in schools or churches where they have their Christmas entertainments. You can hear children sing their Christmas carols and recite passages from the Scriptures, while some tell Christmas stories or recite speeches that they have memorized concerning the meaning of Christmas. The congregation enjoys seeing Christmas plays performed by the pupils of the Sunday schools.

The author has written quite a few plays to convey the spirit of Christmas. Each play has a Christmas message for the audience. Non-Christian parents connected with our schools do not care to go to church, but they like to come to see their own children in our Christmas plays which we hope will touch their hearts.

In order to have a happy Christmas, we have to make people happy during the Christmas season. We encourage people, especially the poorer folks who live in slums, to come to our Christmas entertainments so that they may have a good time. We give to each of the poorer children some useful gifts, such as towels, toothbrushes, soap and used clothes and shoes as well as cakes, candies and oranges.

We have Christmas entertainments for the boat people who live on houseboats, (there are 250,000 people living on houseboats in Hong Kong), for the patients in the hospitals and clinics, for prisoners and coolies. The mission of the United Brethren in Christ has two clinics for poorer people in Hong Kong because medical service is too expensive and they need medical treatment free of charge. Two of our Bible women (Mrs. K. Y. Tse and Miss Y. F. Lum) preach the gospel to the patients who come to our clinics where we can render Christian service to these less fortunate people.

In Hong Kong non-Christian people also celebrate Christmas, without knowing its meaning, by doing Christmas shopping, giving Christmas presents and sending Christmas cards to their relatives and friends. Quite a few shops in Hong Kong are decorated with a Santa Claus, Christmas trees and other colorful decorations. Even stores that sell joss sticks and paper articles for worshipping the dead also sell Christmas cards.

The average Chinese does not understand the meaning of Christmas. As winter solstice is always three days before Christmas, they say that Christmas is the winter solstice for the foreigners. As the Christians have a good time during Christmas, the Chinese who are not Christians want to have a good time during the winter solstice festival too. They celebrate the winter solstice by having better food, such as chicken or ducks in their homes and shops; even the poorest Chinese kills a chicken or duck for the winter solstice festival to avoid being despised by relatives and friends.

So most people in China would say that Christmas is a foreign celebration of winter solstice, not knowing that Christ was born in Bethlehem which is in Asia, and that Jesus is an Asian. If "Asia is for the Asians," why not Jesus Christ for the

Asians? As Christ is an Asian, and since all the great religions in the world have had their origins in Asia (such as Judaism, Christianity, Confucianism, Taoism, Hinduism, Islam or the Moslem religion, Buddhism, Lamaism, and Shintoism) so the Chinese, as Asians, should accept the gospel of Jesus Christ who came to this world to die for all people, including the Asians, of course. As more than half the people in this world live in Asia, it is a pity to see that there are less than twenty-five million Christians in Asia today.

Christmas vacation in China is very short, from one to three days, so that Chinese children do not have a merry Christmas. Most people in China want to celebrate the Chinese New Year (the first day of the first moon) which comes between the end of January and the middle of February, because they have firecrackers for two or more days, and children receive small red envelopes with money to buy firecrackers or toys.

Members of the choir in each church and school go to Christian homes on Christmas eve to sing Christmas carols until three or four o'clock in the morning. In 1937 the author saw a young Chinese mother carrying her one-month-old baby with her to sing in the choir. She was told to return home in order not to catch cold. This shows that the Chinese Christians have genuine love for Christ and are willing to do what they can for Him.

Chinese Christians who are comparatively poor, due to wars, are asked not to spend much money on Christmas cards and gifts for friends and relatives, but to save the money to give to the poorer people. Christ appreciates it if we help the poorer people to celebrate His birthday. As He is the King of kings and Prince of Peace, if we love Him, we should spread the good news of His birth so that those who accept Him as their Savior will have eternal life, which is the best Christmas gift for everyone who believes in Him.

20

How We Can Go Further With Christ in the Publication of Chinese Christian Literature

As CHINESE CHRISTIAN LITERATURE IS SO LIMITED, THERE IS a great demand for good books for Chinese Christians to read. Only about ten percent of the Chinese can read and write and the majority of the Chinese Christians cannot read English. Even most preachers and pastors of churches in Hong Kong and South China cannot read English.

It is therefore a special feature of our Heap Gay Church in Hong Kong to print more books and tracts in Chinese for them to read. At the same time we want the non-Christians who want to study about Christianity to read our books and tracts.

To go further with Christ in the publication of Chinese Christian literature we should write and print as many books and tracts as we can. Good books in English should be translated into Chinese for the Chinese Christians and non-Christians so that they may have a better knowledge of Christianity and the church, that their faith will be strengthened and the lukewarm members of the church be encouraged to render more service to the Master. We also want to reach the non-Christian Chinese with our tracts and books, giving them the Gospel message of salvation and telling more about our Savior.

During the last five years of my ministry in Hong Kong as pastor of the Heap Gay and Zion Churches, I wrote and printed ninety different kinds of tracts and twenty-four books, many of which have been sponsored by the W.M.A. of the United Brethren in Christ and by Christian friends whose names are too numerous to mention.

Our tracts and books have been sent to the overseas Chinese in Macao, Formosa, Japan, Philippines, Indo-China, Indonesia, Burma, Siam, Malaya, Singapore, Mauritius, Honolulu, U.S.A., Canada, Central and South America and Europe. There are over twenty million Chinese living outside of China mainland and we want to reach as many of them as possible. The most economical way of reaching these Chinese is with our printed page.

In Hong Kong, Kowloon and British New Territory we have distributed our tracts and books among the two hundred thousand students and the sixty thousand Christians. We also give our tracts to hotels, hospitals, clinics, stores or shops, restaurants, churches, schools and homes. We distribute them among passengers traveling on ferries across the harbor, and on street cars or trams and buses.

Our Christian workers and the author always carry a good supply of our Chinese Christian literature so that we may give to those who are interested. We have received quite a few letters from our readers who are appreciative of our work and want to read more of our literature.

I was told that one Chinese woman whose attempt to commit suicide was unsuccessful was given some of our tracts to read in the hospital. She received comfort and repented of her sins. She wanted to read more tracts and asked her brother to get them for her from our church.

Dr. S. C. Young, a very earnest Christian in Hong Kong, always carried our tracts in his pockets and briefcase so that he could give them to his patients and to those who are inquirers into the Christian truth.

Pastors of the churches in Hong Kong and Kowloon (there

are more than fifty churches in Hong Kong) and Macao always give our tracts and books to the new converts or candidates who prepare themselves for baptism so that they may study them.

Among the books that we have printed are: Christianity Stands the Tests of Science, in four volumes of ten chapters each; Bible stories for Chinese children, in two volumes of twenty stories in each volume; Bible Characters, in two volumes, chosen from the Old and New Testaments (ten outstanding people in each volume); three volumes of Religious and Christmas One-Act Plays, with six plays in each volume; and the following books for devotional study: (1) Spiritual Milk, (2) Spikenard, (3) The Spiritual World, with one hundred and twenty lessons for Bible study written by the author when he was the principal of the Pui Ching High School in Canton, and (4) eight volumes of sermons, some of which were read over the radio in Hong Kong. In addition to the above, The Prodigal Son, a three-act play and On What Does a Man Live?, a four-act play, a hymnbook in Chinese, English and Romanized Chinese, and a book on nutrition and health have been printed.

We want to continue writing and printing more tracts and books in the near future and ask all those who are interested in our work to pray for our readers so that they will study the Bible and accept Jesus Christ as their Savior.

21

The Chemistry of the Soul

"Who shall change our vile body, that it may be fashioned like unto his glorious body, according to the working whereby he is able even to subdue all things unto himself." (Philippians 3:21.)

"But we all, with open face beholding as in a glass the glory of the Lord, are changed into the same image from glory to glory, even as by the Spirit of the Lord." (II Corinthians 3:18.)

"Behold, I show you a mystery; We shall not all sleep, but we shall all be changed, In a moment, in the twinkling of an eye, at the last trump: for the trumpet shall sound, and the dead shall be raised incorruptible, and we shall be changed. For this corruptible must put on incorruption, and this mortal must put on immortality." (I Corinthians 15:51-53.)

THE ABOVE THREE PASSAGES OF SCRIPTURE DEAL WITH THE chemistry of the soul.

Chemistry is concerned with matter and the changes which it undergoes. In chemistry we study about physical and chemical changes. Changes which occur with the alteration of composition are called chemical changes. Digestion of food, burning of coal, souring of milk, decaying of animal and vegetable matter, rusting of iron, etc., are chemical changes. Chemical changes are always accompanied by liberation or absorption of heat energy. Spiritual changes are accompanied by the energy for Christian service and the passion for souls.

Chemical changes consist of the alteration of composition and chemical properties. A Christian must have spiritual change in virtues and character. "Therefore if any man be in Christ, he is a new creature: old things are passed away; behold, all things are become new."(II Corinthians 5:17.)

In spiritual changes a Christian must be so changed that he is Christ-like. His center of gravity must be changed from self-centeredness to Christ-centeredness. He must give up his own way, his old habits and thoughts, and live God's way every day. Chemical changes are carrying on in the human body all the time. When man dies, chemical changes are still carrying on in the grave. The final change will be at the resurrection when our Lord returns.

In order to understand spiritual changes we should know something about chemical changes. In chemistry we have the following changes:

1. Useless substances are changed to useful compounds.

2. Undesirable and unpleasant substances are purified and refined and changed to useful things.

3. Tasteless and odorless substances are changed into fragrant compounds.

4. Substances from coal tar are changed into beautiful dyes of various colors.

In spiritual changes we have the following results:

1. Sinners and wicked people are born again and are changed by the Holy Spirit into men and women who will live and die for Christ. The disciples of Jesus Christ were changed from cowards and men without sympathy to men of courage and love, willing to sacrifice for the Cause and the extension of God's kingdom. Saul, the persecutor of Christians, was changed

into Paul, the Apostle to the Gentiles. They put on the "new man, which after God is created in righteousness and true holiness" (Ephesians 4:24), and "which is renewed in knowledge after the image of Him that created him." (Colossians 3:10.)

2. The soul is purified by the blood of Jesus Christ. "Unto the pure all things are pure; but unto them that are defiled and unbelieving is nothing pure; but even their mind and conscience is defiled." (Titus 1:15.) "Though your sins be as scarlet, they shall be as white as snow; though they be red like crimson, they shall be as wool." (Isaiah 1:18.)

3. A Christian is changed from a man of whom the Bible says, "Their throat is an open sepulchre; with their tongues they have used deceit; the poison of asps is under their lips" (Romans 3:13), to a man who "maketh manifest the savour of his knowledge by us in every place. For we are unto God a sweet savour of Christ." (II Corinthians 2:14-15.)

Jesus Christ is a chemist of the soul. He can change men if they will accept Him as their Savior. But Jesus Christ is never changed. "Jesus Christ is the same yesterday, and today, and forever." (Hebrews 13:8.) In chemistry a catalyst is never changed. Jesus Christ is a spiritual catalyst.

A Christian who is born again is changed spiritually. "Except a man be born again, he cannot see the kingdom of God." (John 3:3.) Regeneration is a spiritual change. Jesus said, "Blessed are the pure in heart [change of the soul]: for they shall see God." (Matthew 5:8.) Purity in heart means a complete spiritual change of the soul.

Spiritual changes are similar to chemical changes which follow definite principles.

Change from the fleshly to the spiritual—this is a very important spiritual reaction of the soul. Because "that which is born of the flesh is flesh: and that which is born of the Spirit is spirit." (John 3:6.) In Romans 8:9-10 Paul said: "But ye

71

are not in the flesh, but in the Spirit, if so be that the Spirit of God dwell in you. Now if any man have not the Spirit of Christ, he is none of His. And if Christ be in you, the body is dead because of sin; but the Spirit is life because of righteousness."

From selfishness to self-denial. Zaccheus is a good example of this spiritual change. It is a change from egoism to altruism. When Christ entered his house he was converted and saved. He said to the Lord, "Behold, Lord, the half of my goods I give to the poor: and if I have taken any thing from any man by false accusation, I restore him fourfold." (Luke 19:8.) The whole character of Zaccheus was changed. He gave up his own way and followed God's way every day of his spiritual life.

From earthly to heavenly. This is the final change of a Christian at the second coming of the King of kings, and Lord of lords. In I Corinthians 15:50-53 Paul said, "Flesh and blood cannot inherit the kingdom of God; neither doth corruption inherit incorruption . . . and the dead shall be raised incorruptible, and we shall be changed. For this corruptible must put on incorruption, and this mortal must put on immortality."

1. Spiritual interference or hindrance with the growth of our spiritual life can be compared with analytical chemistry. In analytical chemistry, which I have taught for more than thirty years, organic compounds, colloidal substances, silicates, etc., are interfering substances which must be removed before the analysis of certain metals, e.g. aluminum, manganese, etc., can proceed.

In the chemistry of the soul, sin is the interfering substance or hindrance to spiritual growth. Sin must be eliminated from the soul. We should repent and ask God to forgive us.

2. In chemistry we need a catalyst to increase the speed of reactions. The catalyst in our spiritual activities is the Holy Spirit, giving us passion for souls and energy and stimulus to Christian service.

3. Many antiseptics have been discovered in chemistry to

prevent infection. We need a spiritual antiseptic which is the Word of God to eliminate the undesirable elements which interfere with the health of the soul.

4. In chemistry many anesthetic compounds have been discovered to give insensibility to pain. The anesthetic for the soul is faith. A Christian lives by faith and trust in God so that he is not sensitive to all kinds of suffering and persecution for Christ, just like the apostles who "departed from the presence of the council, rejoicing that they were counted worthy to suffer shame for His name." (Acts 5:41.)

Mendelyeev (Russian chemist) discovered the periodic law which helps the chemist and physicist to predict the discovery of new elements and their properties. Paul gave us the spiritual knowledge when he said, "He that is spiritual judgeth all things, yet he himself is judged of no man." (I Corinthians 2:15.)

In chemistry we have the principle of Le Châtelier (French chemist) in connection with chemical equilibrium which is a principle of universal application to systems in equilibrium. It is stated as follows: If a stress is placed upon a system in equilibrium whereby the equilibrium is altered, that change will take place which tends to relieve or neutralize the effect of the added stress.

The stress in spiritual equilibrium is the removal of those things which would react on the virtues of the soul such as temptations, backsliding, heresy, etc.

As in certain chemical reactions, we can carry our spiritual chemical changes to completion by living a separate and holy life so that we can have constant communion with Christ (formation of a gas in a chemical change) or by casting away things which do not please God (formation of a precipitate in a chemical change) or by living a sinless life (formation of un-ionized substances in chemistry).

Chemistry is a practical branch of science. We must experiment in order to find the truth and benefit by it. "O taste and see that the Lord is good: blessed is the man that trusteth in Him." (Psalm 34:8.) We must experiment in prayer with faith and endurance. In the laboratory of life there are ample room and opportunities to perform the tests. In addition to prayer we can experiment in all the things that the Bible tells us to do.

This is a changing world. We must change in order to adjust to our environment. A Christian should have change (for the better) in his spiritual life.

Our physical bodies are made up of electrons, protons and neutrons put together to form elements. We find sixteen or more of these elements in appreciable amounts in the human body. If we were to analyze the body of a person weighing one hundred and forty pounds, we would find that it contains ten gallons of water. There is enough fat for seven bars of soap, enough carbon for nine thousand lead pencils, enough phosphorus to make twenty-two hundred matches, enough iron to make a medium-sized nail, etc. But is this all we are? Are we worth only the eighty-seven cents the chemicals in our bodies would cost?

The Bible tells us that the Lord "formed man of the dust of the earth [sixteen or more elements] and breathed into his nostrils the breath of life, and man became a living soul." Our souls are so precious that God sent His only Son to die for us.

We do not know what the elements of our souls are. Our souls need nourishing food. The food for our souls is the Word of God. With proper food for the soul one can grow spiritually and bear the fruit of the Holy Spirit, "love, joy, peace, long-suffering, gentleness, goodness, faith, meekness, temperance." (Galatians 5:22-23.)

God created man out of the dust of the earth. The physical life will be ours for a short period of time but spiritual life can be ours for all eternity.

To have this spiritual life we must be cleansed from sin, and this is accomplished only through the sacrifice of Jesus Christ, the Son of God, who died to save us and to redeem our precious souls.

In our blood we have substances called buffers which are important to the living organism. Our blood is buffered or protected. By choosing our food wisely (eating more fruits and vegetables and less meat) our blood can be maintained at a slightly alkaline (not acid) condition, a slight change in which results in serious illness or even death.

Similarly, in the chemistry of the soul, the blood of our Lord Jesus Christ acts as a buffer to all believers. We who are Christians are protected from spiritual illness or eternal death.

Summarizing: We must remember that our souls need nourishing food for maintenance and growth. Souls should be saved by believing in Jesus and being purified by His blood. Souls should be inspired for service by the Holy Spirit so that when the Lord returns, our vile bodies will be changed into incorruptible bodies to live forever with the King of kings.

Let us submit our souls to these spiritual changes by the power of God in obedience to His laws of change.

22

Spiritual Engineering

"According to the grace of God which is given unto me, as a wise masterbuilder, I have laid the foundation, and another buildeth thereon. But let every man take heed how he buildeth there upon. For other foundation can no man lay than that is laid, which is Jesus Christ. Now if any man build upon this foundation gold, silver, precious stones, wood, hay, stubble; Every man's work shall be made manifest: for the day shall declare it, because it shall be revealed by fire; and the fire shall try every man's work of what sort it is. If any man's work abide which he hath built thereupon, he shall receive a reward. If any man's work shall be burned, he shall suffer loss: but he himself shall be saved: yet so as by fire." (I Corinthians 3:10-15.)

THESE VERSES OF THE SCRIPTURES TELL US THAT PAUL IS A spiritual engineer and a wise masterbuilder. From his rich experiences he has given us a spiritual lesson that in construction we should select the best building materials which must also be fireproof.

The Lord advised us to build on the surest foundation. He said, "Therefore whosoever heareth these sayings of mine, and doeth them, I will liken him unto a wise man, which built his house upon a rock: And the rain descended, and the floods came, and the winds blew, and beat upon that house; and it fell not: for it was founded upon a rock." (Matthew 7:24-25.) From this we learn that building on a good foundation and using the best materials are essential so that it can stand all kinds of tests, even as the strength of materials must meet certain tests in civil engineering.

Hearing the Word of God and doing His will is comparable to a wise man's building his house on a rock which can stand earthquake and storm and shocks. Christians should stand against spiritual tests in the form of temptations, persecutions, suffering for the cause of Christ. By doing as Christ wants them to do they can stand firm, unmovable, for they have built upon a strong foundation—the Lord Jesus Christ.

There are two kinds of construction: permanent and temporary. For permanent construction, we should use the best, the strongest, and the most reliable materials. For example, we use steel, concrete, alloys, stone, brick in the construction of bridges, buildings, tunnels, etc. These building materials are expensive but they are strong and reliable. For temporary buildings, Paul said that wood, hay, and stubble, which are not fireproof, may be used.

In China and in some places in Hong Kong and Kowloon, poorer people use palm leaves, bamboo, etc., for building huts, which catch fire very easily. On Christmas eve, 1953, seven thousand of these huts were destroyed by fire, so that seventy thousand people were left homeless.

We all know that for the construction of bridges, skyscrapers, tunnels, subways, railroads, dams, airplanes, automobiles, etc., we should use materials which will withstand shock and strain, and which are weatherproof. Buildings should be able to stand against fire, wind, flood, earthquake and termites if they are to remain standing for centuries, like the pyramids in Egypt or the Great Wall and the pagodas in China. The ancient people took pains to use the very best materials.

In spiritual engineering we should also use the best materials, and in building Christian character we should select the virtues which will withstand the following tests: temptations by the devil, trial and persecution, personal loss, misunderstanding and criticism by others, disappointments, etc. Can we stand these tests as well as Job?

We must build on a solid foundation. Jesus said, "And every one that heareth these sayings of mine, and doeth them not, shall be likened unto a foolish man, which built his house upon the sand: And the rain descended, and the floods came, and the winds blew, and beat upon that house; and it fell: and great was the fall of it." (Matthew 7:26-27.)

Is not this a total loss? Why not avoid this catastrophe by building on a solid spiritual foundation which will last eternally?

All engineers know that for bridge construction one should select steel which is free from small amounts of carbon, silicon and phosphorus, as these tend to make steel brittle, causing it to lose its tensile strength. So our spiritual building materials should be free from sin and spiritual defects which weaken the soul. Paul said: "That he might present it to himself a glorious church, not having spot, or wrinkle, or any such thing; but that it should be holy and without blemish." (Ephesians 5:27.) This is the spiritual engineering required in kingdom building. We know that sin and evil habits and thoughts are the bad spots or wrinkles which should be eliminated in Christian character building so that there will be no blemishes in our spiritual make-up.

In spiritual engineering, if there are such defects as hidden sin, disastrous results will come to pass, for Jesus said, "There is nothing covered, that shall not be revealed; and hid, that shall not be known. (Matthew 10:26.) Paul said, "Every man's work shall be made manifest: for the day shall declare it, because it shall be revealed by fire; and the fire shall try every man's work of what sort it is." (I Corinthians 3:13.) Our work will come to naught if we use defective materials.

Several years ago a new building collapsed in Hong Kong, killing many people. This was due to defective materials used by the contractor.

Jesus pointed out that hypocrisy and false pretense are defective materials in kingdom building. That is why we must be sincere and honest in our service and work for the extension of His kingdom. All Christians should guard against the use of defective materials.

Realizing the importance of building on a strong foundation, Solomon said, "As the whirlwind passeth, so is the wicked no more: but the righteous is an everlasting foundation." (Proverbs 10:25.)

In Psalm 37:17-40 David said, ". . . but the Lord upholdeth the righteous. . . . Their inheritance shall be for ever. They shall not be ashamed in the evil time: and in the days of famine they shall be satisfied. . . . The steps of a good man are ordered by the Lord: and he delighteth in his way. Though he fall, he shall not be utterly cast down: for the Lord upholdeth him with his hand. I have been young, and now am old; yet have I not seen the righteous forsaken, nor his seed begging bread. . . . But the salvation of the righteous is of the Lord: he is their strength in the time of trouble. And the Lord shall help them, and deliver them: he shall deliver them from the wicked, and save them, because they trust in him."

So, trusting in God is the best and safest thing a Christian can do. David said, "The Lord is my rock, and my fortress, and my deliverer; the God of my rock; in him will I trust: he is my shield, and the horn of my salvation, my high tower, and my refuge, my savior; thou savest me from violence." (II Samuel 22:2-3.) Can we put our trust in God as David did? Only trust in God can make us calm in the atomic age in which we live today.

Jesus said, "For which of you, intending to build a tower, sitteth not down first, and counteth the cost, whether he have sufficient to finish it? Lest haply, after he hath laid the foundation, and is not able to finish it, all that behold it begin to mock him. Saying, This man began to build, and was not able to finish." (Luke 1:28-30.) So in spiritual construction we should have a plan and count the cost so that with God's help we shall be able to accomplish that which we intend to build for the kingdom of God.

From his rich experience, Paul said, "Laying up in store for themselves a good foundation against the time to come, that they may lay hold on eternal life." (I Timothy 6:19.) Rendering service for Christ and living for Him will enable a Christian to lay up in store a good foundation in Christian character and kingdom building which will last forever.

There is nothing in this world which can be considered permanent. Paul taught us to build that which will last eternally. He said, "For we know that if our earthly house of this tabernacle were dissolved, we have a building of God, an house not made with hands, eternal in the heavens." (II Corinthians 5:1.)

What is more permanent than this? He also said in Ephesians 2:20-21, "And are built upon the foundation of the apostles and prophets, Jesus Christ himself being the chief corner stone; In whom all the building fitly framed together groweth unto an holy temple in the Lord." This is spiritual construction or engineering which all Christians must practice.

Remember what Paul said in I Corinthians 3:16-17, "Know ye not that ye are the temple of God, and that the Spirit of God dwelleth in you? If any man defile the temple of God, him shall God destroy; for the temple of God is holy, which temple ye are." know ye not that your body is the temple of the Holy Ghost.

Study what Paul said in I Corinthians 6:19-20, "What?

80

know ye not that your body is the temple of the Holy Ghost which is in you, which ye have of God, and ye are not your own? For ye are bought with a price: therefore glory God in your body, and in your spirit, which are God's." These two verses show that we belong to God and that we should take good care of our bodies and souls.

Paul said in II Corinthians 6:16, ". . . for ye are the temple of the living God; as God hath said, I will dwell in them, and walk in them; and I will be their God, and they shall be my people." So we should keep our bodies and souls holy, for God is holy.

A Chinese proverb tells us that "to take care of the health (the body) is to honor one's father and mother (or be filial to them)." So in taking good care of our bodies and souls, we are honoring God, our Creator and Savior. Our bodies are spiritual dwelling places changed by the Spiritual Engineer and Master builder, our Lord Jesus Christ. Paul told us that since we belong to Christ, no one can destroy our spiritual houses wherein the Lord dwells and which He will keep forever.

In this world new buildings are being erected in every country and gigantic engineering projects are being erected. These help us to understand the principle of spiritual engineering or kingdom building in which every Christian should be interested and have a part—building holy temples for the Holy Spirit to dwell in and constructing spiritual engineering projects for the advancement of God's kingdom.

Can we put up a new spiritual building for God?

By keeping our bodies healthy and holy and winning souls to Christ, we may have a part in kingdom building which will be carried on as long as we live and until the Lord returns.

23

Self-Exaltation and Humiliation

THE TEACHING OF HUMILIATION IS EMPHASIZED BY CONFUCIUS, Mencius and other Chinese philosophers and teachers as this is considered a good virtue. A Chinese proverb tells us, "Humility receives benefit, while self-exaltation brings destruction."

Jesus Christ taught His disciples that "Whosoever shall exalt himself shall be abased; and he that shall humble himself shall be exalted."

Why does Christ place so much emphasis on this virtue? We are told that the Pharisees made broad their phylacteries and enlarged the borders of their garments. They "love the uppermost rooms at feasts, and the chief seats in the synagogues, and greetings in the markets, and to be called of men, Rabbi." (Matthew 23:5-7.)

Jesus saw the self-exaltation and hypocrisy of the Pharisees and religious leaders of His days. He did not want His disciples to follow their bad examples. However, to a certain extent, His disciples got the bad habit from them so that "by the way they disputed among themselves who should be the greatest." (Mark 9:34.) So He spoke two parables to show the importance of humiliation.

"When thou art bidden of any man to a wedding, sit not down in the highest room; lest a more honorable man than thou be bidden of him. And he that bade thee and him come and say to thee, Give this man place; and thou begin with shame to take the lowest room. But when thou art bidden, go and sit down in the lowest room; that when he that bade thee cometh, he may say unto thee, Friend, go up higher: then shalt thou have worship in the presence of them that sit at meat with thee. For whosoever exalteth himself shall be abased; and he that humbleth himself shall be exalted." (Luke 14:8-11.)

"And Jesus spake this parable unto certain which trusted in themselves that they were righteous, and despised others. Two men went up into the temple to pray; the one a Pharisee, and the other a publican. The Pharisee stood and prayed thus with himself, God, I thank Thee, that I am not as other men are, extortioners, unjust, adulterers, or even as this publican. I fast twice in the week. I give tithes of all that I possess. And the publican, standing afar off, would not lift up so much as his eyes unto heaven, but smote upon his breast, saying, God be merciful to me a sinner. I tell you, this man went down to his house justified rather than the other; for every one that exalteth himself shall be abased; and he that humbleth himself shall be exalted." (Luke 18:9-14.)

There are three reasons why Jesus and the Chinese philosophers lay so much emphasis on teaching the importance of humiliation.

1. Self-exaltation is a hindrance to progress.

When Socrates, an Athenian idealist philosopher (470-399 B.C.) was asked, "Were you born a super-man," he replied, "No, I am just an ordinary man. One thing I differ from others. I know that I am ignorant." One summer he built a very small house, the smallest one ever built by any man. When asked why he, being a great man, built such a small house, he said, "Inside my little house, I am great, but when I get out of my small house, I feel small." He felt that he was ignorant, so he humbled himself. Feeling small, he encouraged himself to have progress and gradually became one of the greatest philosophers who ever lived.

Confucius (550-477 B.C.) had the same spirit of humility. He said, "I will not be concerned at men's not knowing me; I will be concerned at my own want of ability. . . . In letters I am perhaps equal to other men, but the character of the superior man carrying out in his conduct what he professes, is what I have not yet attained to. . . . Now the man of distinction is solid and straightforward, and loves righteousness. He examines people's words and looks at their countenances. He is anxious to humble himself to others. Such a man will be distinguished in the country: he will be distinguished in his clan."

2. Self-exaltation will lead to failure.

We know that real success depends upon two things:

(a) Mutual cooperation.

(b) Carefulness in our work.

A person who exalts himself would not consider his own faults or mistakes. He would not forgive others. "They behold the mote that is in their brother's eyes." How can such a man co-operate with others? Certainly no one wants to work with him.

Secondly, one who is careless in his work, may think that he is right. He would not accept any suggestion, advice or criticism of others. Thinking that he alone is right and that others are wrong, he would not make any correction or improvement. He would not even repent or feel sorry for what he has done. How could he trust in God? If one would humble himself before God, he would respect others and listen to advice and instruction. Confucius said, "When I walk along with two others, they may serve as my teachers."

In proverbs we are told that "When pride cometh, then cometh shame: but with the lowly is wisdom." (Proverbs 11:2.) "By humility and the fear of the Lord are riches, and honor, and life." (Proverbs 22:4.) James said, "Humble yourself in the sight of the Lord, and He shall lift you up" (James 4:10) while Peter said, ". . . be clothed with humility: for God resisteth the proud, and giveth grace to the humble." (I Peter 5:5.) "Before destruction the heart of man is haughty, and before honor is humility." (Proverbs 18:12.)

3. Self-exaltation leads to the sad course of forsaking God. It tends to make one have too much self-confidence and to forsake God, like the prodigal son. Atheists behave like this.

There are people who ignore the existence of God, and would do as they please. In the Old Testament we have the story of Nebuchadnezzar who exalted himself, because of his victories and accomplishments. God caused him to have a strange dream that troubled him, because he was not willing to believe in the great God who is over all. Daniel was asked to tell him the meaning of his dream. He spoke bravely to the king and said, "This great tree which you have seen means you, for you have become a great king. And the meaning of that voice which you heard crying out that the great tree should be cut down is that you will lose your kingdom for seven years and go out from men to live among the beasts of the field. You shall eat grass like an ox, and the dew of heaven shall be upon you. But when you humble yourself and believe that God rules in the kingdom of earth, giving them to whosoever He pleases, then you shall be restored to your kingdom." One year later his dream was fulfilled, and he was driven from men, and did eat grass as oxen, and his body was wet with the dew of heaven, till his hairs were grown like eagles' feathers, and his nails like birds' claws.

When Nebuchadnezzar was brought low, he repented and he praised and extolled and honored "the King of heaven (God), all whose works are truth, and His ways judgment: and those that walk in pride He is able to abase." (Daniel 4:37.) This is his humiliation.

Humiliation does not mean that one has to be a slave and yield to his conqueror. It does not mean that he has to remain forever in a low position. It is a spiritual virtue, when one is in his best mood or disposition. Christ teaches us to be humble, gentle and polite. We should listen to suggestions and criticisms and warnings of those who are wiser and more experienced than we.

To humble oneself is to seek advancement in knowledge, be willing to serve God and men.

Take the case of John, the Baptist. See how humble he was. He said, "I indeed baptize you with water unto repentance, but he that cometh after me, is mightier than I, whose shoes I am not worthy to bear." (Matthew 3:11.) In John 3:30 he said, "Jesus must increase, but I must decrease." This shows his humility.

When Thomas Edison was introduced as a speaker at a science meeting, he was given credit as one of the greatest inventors that ever lived. He replied that he was not a great inventor and told the audience that God was the only inventor. He was certainly very humble and spent his life humbly in search of scientific truth.

A story was told of a Chinese patriot who was eager to get rid of the first and cruel emperor Chun. He was unsuccessful and felt disappointed. One day while he was walking on a stone bridge, he found an old man, Wong, who dropped one of his shoes. Chang immediately went under the bridge to pick up the shoe and put it on the foot of the old man who was an authority in military tactics. He was so pleased with Chang that he gave him his book on military science and asked him to study it. Chang went home and studied the book and got many good things out of it. This enabled him to help Lew Pong to get rid of the cruel emperor. If Chang did not humble himself, he would not have received aid from the old man to fulfill his dream.

Jesus Christ set us a very good sample in teaching His disciples a lesson of humility by washing His disciples' feet. He said, "If I then, your Lord and Master, have washed your feet; ye also ought to wash one another's feet. For I have given you an example, that ye should do as I have done to you." (John 13:14-15.)

Paul who had a personal experience of Christ gave us his impression of Him for he said, "Let this mind be in you, which was also in Christ Jesus: Who . . . took upon Him the form of a servant. . . . And being found in fashion as a man, He humbled Himself, and became obedient unto death, even the death of the cross. Wherefore God also hath highly exalted Him, and given Him a name which is above every name: That at the name of Jesus every knee should bow. . . . And that every tongue should confess that Jesus Christ is Lord, to the glory of God the Father." (Philippians 2:5-11.) Certainly Christ is our example of humiliation and God's exaltation.

24

A Retrospect

THE FIRST PROTESTANT MISSIONARY TO COME TO CHINA WAS Dr. Robert Morrison, who came to Canton, South China, from London, England, in 1807. Being the first Protestant missionary to China, he had a very hard time, not only in learning the Chinese language, but in translating the dictionary and Bible into Chinese. He labored for twenty-seven years in China and won only seven souls to Christ. He died on August 1, 1934 and was buried in Macao, a Portuguese colony, fifty miles west of Hong Kong, which is a British colony.

When I was principal of the Pui Ching High School in Macao in 1942, I visited Dr. Morrison's grave.

My grandfather, on my mother's side, Rev. M. Wong, was saved in California about 1860 (he died when my mother was thirteen years old). At that time there were about three thousand Chinese Christians in China. In spite of persecution my grandfather stood for Christ. He was the first ordained Chinese Baptist pastor in China. His son, Rev. N. T. Wong (my uncle), was also an ordained Baptist pastor, while his grandson-in-law, Rev. Moy Ling (Mrs. Moy Ling is my cousin), and his grandson (Y. T. Chiu) are ordained ministers. Thus salvation through the Lord Jesus Christ came to our family through the missionary work of Dr. Robert Morrison who sowed the seed of the Gospel in China which bore fruit in 1814 and multiplied one thousand fold so that today there are approximately three million Christians in China.

The first school for girls was organized by missionaries who had done much to eradicate evil customs in China. My mother, my wife and her mother, aunts and sisters, my three sisters, and my three daughters—all studied in schools founded by missionaries. Even in days of old, my mother, who was born in 1865, and my mother-in-law, who was born in 1871, never had their feet bound. We have learned to live the Christian way of life.

My mother taught me to pray and to read the Bible when I was a boy. My father, who was ordained as a deacon of the Baptist church, in Hong Kong, taught me to sing and brought me to the Sunday school and church when I was six years old. I remember my father told me that as a young man in the U. S. he used to sing in churches when he was in Portland, Oregon. He had a good baritone voice. He often sang in churches in Hong Kong when I played the organ for him.

Being an earnest Christian, my father did his best to give his eight children college educations. Two of his children (the author and his younger brother) received their Ph.D. degrees. He sent four of his five sons to be educated in this country and in England. My younger brother Yan Kwong has taught mathematics at St. Paul's College in Hong Kong since 1916. Another younger brother Yan Tak is a barrister in Hong Kong. He is an authority in Chinese and international law.

My parents were married in Canton, China, and when I was three years old my father brought his family to Hong Kong, where he worked as a pharmaceutical chemist and later in business (shipping), at which he earned much money. Although he was a rich man before World War I, my father was very economical so that he could send his eight children to schools and higher institutions of learning. Six of my younger brothers and sisters have been Christian educators.

My father passed to his eternal reward on March 3, 1921. He was treasurer and deacon of the Baptist Church in Hong Kong prior to his death and preached at the prayer meeting of his church a few days before his passing away. I am indebted to him for my education, training, encouragement and advice. He was interested in my work and welfare and gave me some good advice just the day before he died.

I am grateful and thankful to God for a good father, a good mother, and a faithful wife who has helped me a lot.

We had a family altar in our home and spent much time in prayer. We know that prayer which involves spiritual reactions produces spiritual changes. This explains why "prayer changes things." In life's laboratory one has to perform experiments in prayer. God hears our prayers. Just as chemical reactions work according to scientific laws, prayers are effectual according to the will of God.

I was surprised when, as a young man, some of my friends told me that I could not live up to the age of fifty and that I would have no children. I prayed to God to give me longevity of life that I might have more time to serve Him and that I would not be considered "unfilial." As Mencius (372-289 B.C., a teacher of Confucianism) said, "There are three things which are unfilial, and to have no posterity is the greatest of them."

God has answered my prayers, giving me children and grandchildren and I pray that they all will serve the Lord faithfully.

My mother told me many times that she prayed for me three times a day. My wife also prays for me and many friends told me that they prayed for me and my family during the war. I know that these precious prayers have been answered, for God knows our needs and has taken good care of us.

When Wellington, my elder son, was three years old my wife and I thought that he could not live. One night when he was unconscious we all knelt and prayed for him earnestly. God answered our prayers and spared his life. He was so weak after his long illness that my wife brought him to a missionary altar, where a missionary in his ministry of divine healing prayed for him. In a short time Wellington regained his health and became strong and intelligent. When he was a senior in Lingnan University he won the first prize in biology in a competitive examination among all the colleges and universities in China. He was awarded a prize by the Secretary of Education. He was an honor student when he received his B.S. degree in 1941 and was elected a member of Phi Tau Phi (honor society) at Lingnan University and later in 1950 a member of Sigma Xi (honor society) at the University of California in Berkeley, California, where he received his Ph.D. in biochemistry in 1951. This shows how God answers prayer.

We were in Hong Kong during the eighteen days of fighting from December 7 to December 25, 1941, when Hong Kong was captured by the Japanese. As a matter of precaution, we had to put reinforcements in our windows and doors with strong boards. There were ninety-eight people in our mission school. While we were kneeling in prayer one bomb fell about two hundred yards from our school and a piece of shrapnel weighing almost five pounds pierced through our reinforced window and nearly hit a boy. We were greatly frightened. Many bullets were aimed at our reinforced doors and windows, but thank God, no one got hurt.

We had a hard time getting food to feed so many people during and after the war in Hong Kong. Our workers and teachers had to expose themselves to danger, going out during the bombing to purchase food which was scarce and expensive. Banks were closed. In order to obtain money we had to sell all our belongings.

My wife received divine wisdom to cope with the Japanese soldiers who came asking for watches, fountain pens, etc. She wrote her answers in Chinese, "We have given you all our watches, and fountain pens, etc." Her cousin wrote, "You have destroyed my house and taken all our precious belongings. What more do you want?" One Japanese soldier wrote in reply, "We are in sympathy with you." (Many Japanese soldiers could read Chinese writings.)

Several times Japanese soldiers wanted to occupy our school building in Hong Kong, but the Lord answered our prayers, so that for six months after our school was closed (all Christian schools in Hong Kong were closed) we used our school building to accommodate the refugees.

When I was walking in Hong Kong with my brother-in-law and a friend of ours shortly after the Japanese occupation by the Army, we were severely beaten by the Japanese soldiers, just because we did not salute one of the soldiers. The wounds on our bodies lasted several months. We thanked God that they did not torture us, but we were told that many were tortured for similar "offense" or violation of their regulations. We were thankful to God for His care again.

In February 1942 Mrs. Chiu, Christine, my daughter, and Florence, my niece, went back to Canton to stay for one year to render Christian service to the victims of war.

On June 11, 1942 I left Hong Kong with my mother-in-law, Bessie (my youngest daughter), Paul (my younger son) and Willa (my niece who was nine years old) for Macao (Portuguese colony) where I served as principal of the Pui Ching High School. After staying nearly four months in Macao, I was asked by the board of trustees of the school to go to Ping Shek in "free" China to visit our Pui Luen High School where I was also principal. It took me two weeks to reach my destination. At first I wanted to ask Mr. C. S. Lee, my secretary, to accompany me, but he was too nervous to take a strenuous and very perilous journey. So he refused to accompany me. Before I left

Macao, I said to Mr. Lee, "You have been working for ten years in a Christian school, and you have not accepted Christ as your Savior. I sincerely hope that you will be a Christian soon." Mr. Lee replied, "I want to wait until the war is over, then I shall be baptized on V-J day." Unfortunately Mr. Lee died just before the end of the war, and he was not saved.

When I reached Kukong, the provincial war capital of Kwangtung, I went to visit Lingnan University which was located in a village near Kukong. Dr. Y. L. Lee, president of the university, told me that my wife and Christine, my daughter, had been "captured" by the Japanese. He advised me to go to Canton immediately to "rescue" them. I was rather excited and did not know what to do. After much prayer, I felt that it would not be wise for me to go to Canton, as it would not be possible for me to do anything for my family if they were "prisoners." So I decided not to go but to attend my duty of visiting our schools in Ping Shek and Kweilin and to report the work to the board of trustees in Kweilin.

One month later I returned safely to Macao before Christmas, 1942. To my surprise I was thrilled to see my wife and daughter standing at the pier to see me. Immediately I knew that God had answered my prayers. My wife told me they had never been "captured" by the Japanese who were very kind to them, giving them food and supplies and helping them to get a permit to come to Macao from Canton. So I have learned to trust in God and not to pay attention to rumors.

In the spring of 1943, my wife and Christine went on separate tours to Ping Shek in "free" China. Mrs. Chiu took Florence, my niece, and a few Christian workers with her. They experienced bombing by enemy planes on their way and only reached their destination after three weeks of a strenuous and nerve-wracking journey. God answered prayers and gave them mercy during this perilous journey.

93

As principal of two high schools I had to make three tours to "free" China to supervise the Pui Luen schools. In July 1943 I brought Bessie, my daughter, and Paul, my younger son, and Willa, my niece, to Ping Shek so that they could study at our Pui Luen school. Thank God that none of them missed school during the war. They all were graduated from high school at the age of eighteen while many hundreds of thousands could not go to school during the long war.

When I was in my native village (Sun Wui, which is noted for sweet oranges) a cousin of mine came to see me and offered to help me by getting some soldiers to protect us on the way. I thanked him for his kind offer, but I knew that we should not trust only in men, for divine protection is much better. He argued that we had to go through dangerous territories and the children might be kidnapped. But we had complete confidence in God.

Before we came to the "dangerous spots" we met some government soldiers, and we all thanked God for unforeseen care and protection.

At Ching Yuen we nearly fell into a "trap" of kidnappers, but we followed the advice and warning of a friend, who was formerly a Y.M.C.A. secretary in Canton. Finally we reached our destination safely in twenty-three days in spite of an epidemic of cholera during which hundreds of people died, and we had to boil our drinking water from a dirty river.

We were inoculated against typhoid before we left Macao, but we had to do it over again before we could purchase our tickets on the railroad from Kukong to Ping Shek. Bessie, my daughter, nearly fainted, but after our prayer for her she felt better. We had a happy family reunion in Ping Shek.

Since my brother-in-law (Mr. W. J. Wen), who was in Calcutta, India, advised me to send his mother and my whole family to "free" China, I sent my mother-in-law to Ping Shek in the summer of 1943 with a friend. In spite of her kidney disease and diabetes, she safely reached her destination where my wife took care of her.

I returned alone to Macao, safely going through "occupied" territory. I had to go through Canton. I was glad to find that everywhere I went, I was treated kindly by the Japanese soldiers and police.

When I reached Canton on August 31, 1943, after an absence of five years, my mother died in Hong Kong at the age of 78. She was buried beside my father in a Christian cemetery. As I could not send money back to Hong Kong, one of my relatives paid all her funeral expenses.

When I reached Macao on September 2, 1943 I received a telegram from my brother Kwong in Hong Kong, telling me of the death of my mother. One teacher was surprised to find that I carried on my duty as principal and "did not mourn for my mother." I told him that my duty was more important, and that since my mother had gone to her eternal reward and some day I would see her in heaven, what was the use of having a "month of mourning" and neglecting my duty? If it were not for God's help, I would not be so calm in time of distress, trouble, and danger. One fellow passenger in "occupied" territory talked about me. "See, that old man was not a bit nervous as he was inspected by Japanese soldiers."

As the trustees of our high school wanted me to go to Ping Shek and one of them promised to be acting principal in Macao, I took a different route to Ping Shek. Realizing that God had protected me during two previous tours in "free" China, a Christian teacher, Mrs. Choey, and her two small children and her sister accompanied me to Kweilin to join her husband, who was a former student of mine in Lingnan University, where I taught chemistry for twenty-seven years.

Mrs. Choey worried about our safety, and her children cried

quite frequently during the long journey of two weeks. As we had to go through "forbidden occupied" territory, she asked me whether she should use large bath towels to cover the heads of her children to deaden the noise so that the Japanese could not hear the crying. I said to her, "This is not faith, and it might kill your children. You should trust in God and pray continuously." When it was quite dark, (an hour after sunset), we went through dangerous waters for forty-five minutes. I told Mrs. Choey to put her children to sleep. They slept soundly when our boat passed through the "forbidden" territory. When we were out of reach of machine guns, the two children cried loudly. The fellow passengers were thrilled and said that the two children had behaved wonderfully, not knowing that this is God's answer to prayer.

I spent fifteen months with my wife and my two youngest children in Ping Shek. I had to spend much time going to different places to raise money for the school. It was a very difficult task, but the Lord helped me and gave me travel mercy. On my birthday in April 1944, when I was in Kukong, I experienced one of the worst air raids. I thought I would die on my birthday. I prayed that the Lord's will be done and my life was spared. The Commissioner of Education wanted all schools to be moved to Lin Hsien, where it was considered safer. I had to find money to meet our needs. We had to travel in crowded buses which used charcoal to generate carbon monoxide as fuel because gasoline was too expensive and hard to get. Buses were so slow that it took us eight to ten hours to reach our destination. After having spent three months in Lin Hsien we moved our school back to Ping Shek where we re-opened our school in the fall. Less than one hundred students came back and we got along smoothly until the final examinations at the end of the semester when the Japanese came shortly after Christmas.

In January 1945 Ping Shek was occupied by the Japanese.

I was in Kukong at that time, and our school had to move to Lok Cheung. Three weeks later, Lok Cheung was occupied by the Japanese and my mother-in-law died on February 1, 1945. We could not find a casket, so we "borrowed" a wardrobe in which to bury her. In 1948 Mrs. Chiu went to Lok Cheung to take the remains of her mother for burial in a Christian cemetery in Canton, China. This was a very dangerous journey for her, but God gave her divine protection in answer to our prayers. We spent almost three months in Lok Cheung and had a very hard time. One day Paul, my youngest child, was so frightened that he said to his mother, "Mother, I wish Jesus would soon return. I am afraid to stay in this terrible place." His mother told him to pray and ask God to help us.

One day when a Japanese threatened to kill me with a sword, I prayed and he changed his mind. One Japanese soldier took my heavy overcoat. In fifteen minutes he returned with my bunch of keys. I talked to him in writing, "You are a young soldier. How can you fight with a heavy overcoat? Let me give you a top coat." One soldier talked to him, "Give back the heavy overcoat to the old man. Do not take anything from him." A few days later we were astonished to see these soldiers bring presents to our younger children. They were fond of Paul, my son, and came to play with him occasionally.

We did not know how to get out of Lok Cheung. After much prayer, I decided to leave Lok Cheung with two students, one of whom later became my son-in-law. We moved our whole school to Yu Cheng in Hunan province where one of the parents of our students was very kind to us and gave us money and rice to take care of our school for nine months, when we reopened our schools in Yu-cheng, (Hunan), Kian and Nan-chang in Kiangsi province. Being short of money, we sought to borrow $200,000 (Chinese currency), equivalent to $200 U.S., from the Bank of Hunan, but our case was turned down. We could only bring our problem to God in prayer. Then Christine, my daughter, and her two classmates opened a restaurant and a bakery. One medical doctor loaned us $5,000 Chinese currency to start with, and we made $360,000 (Chinese currency), enough to meet our needs for several months.

We were short of money again. So I wrote to the Relief Committee in Chung King, the war capital, for help, but instead of a favorable reply, the general secretary wrote thus, "I do not see why you moved your school so far from Canton and wonder how you can return home safely."

We had no money to bring our teachers and their families and students back to Canton. After much prayer, a friend loaned us $200,000 Chinese currency (equivalent to $200 U.S.), and after twenty-six days of strenuous journey we returned to Canton safely. We hired three large boats to hold sixty-six persons and it took us two weeks to go from Nanchang to Kian where we waited to charter three buses to take us back to Canton. We were told to wait because all buses had been held up by bandits and robbed during the last three days. After prayer we felt that trusting in the Lord, we had better start our perilous journey. It took us three days to go from Kian to Kukong by bus. We prayed during our trip and we thanked God that nothing happened as several thousand soldiers were on the road when we traveled.

In Kukong we hired two large boats to take us back to Canton and after seven days we reached our destination safely. During the long journey from Nanching to Canton none of us, including a one-year-old baby who had been in a hospital six months earlier, got sick. There were bandits and a cyclone, but God gave us a safe journey home.

For four years we could not hear from Dorothy, my eldest daughter, and Wellington, my elder son, who were studying at P.U.M.A. (Peking Union Medical College), built by the Rockefeller Foundation. When the medical college was closed my children went to Shanghai where Dorothy completed her study and received her M.D. in 1945 and worked in the Red Cross hospital, while Wellington worked as an analytical chemist doing work on sewage disposal. My wife and I were thrilled to hear from our oldest children.

Finally, after years of anxiety and worries we had a happy family reunion in Canton in the spring of 1946, when my elder children returned home safely and we stayed together happily for seven months. This was the only time we could have a family reunion since 1940 and we are at a loss to know when we shall have our family reunion again.

Mrs. Chiu often told her friends and relatives not to worry about her, and she told them "to change all worries into prayers." She is willing to do everything she can to serve the Lord. For over forty years we have experienced blessings in "the garden of prayer." It is wonderful to see the results of prayers, most of which have been answered. Why should we not continue to pray for the rest of our lives that greater things may be accomplished in soul winning and kingdom building and that we may go "further with Christ" in our Christian activities?

During the last seven years our work in Hong Kong was done by faith and prayers. We now have a membership of about three hundred souls in our Heap Gay Church and one hundred and five members in our Zion Church in Hong Kong. On December 18, 1955, thirty-two persons (including two teachers, twenty-eight students and two servants) were baptized in our Heap Gay Church in Hong Kong. Mrs. Roberta Granaas and Mrs. May Howard of Burbank and Pixley, California, visited our churches and saw our workers in action in Hong Kong from March 9 to the 20th, 1956. Many pictures were taken when they were with our congregations and workers. The two lady visitors were interested in our school, clinical work, and our church work—all done in answer to prayers. The work has been carried on during the last thirty-two years. Wherever we have gone we have felt that the Lord has been with us. We want to solicit more "prayer warriors." Won't you readers join with us in prayer so that we can do our work as faithfully as Nehemiah, who set us a good example? He was a pioneer prayer warrior. Many wonderful things will be accomplished for Christ through prayers.

As principal of one of the largest high schools in China and president of the oldest theological seminary in China, it was not always easy for me to render my service. But the Lord gave me wisdom to cope with the situations. I acted as peace-maker between two teachers who fought. They refused to be friends again and told me that they would rather die than be reconciled. Even the student pastor refused to act as peace-maker. After much prayer I brought them together reluctantly at first, but finally they shook hands and apologized. Such things can only be done by much prayer and personal interview. Through prayer I often settled disputes among our staff and trouble-makers in our school. I went once to an "armed" staff meeting where trouble was expected. But through the help of God nothing happened, to the surprise of quite a few teachers.

Through prayer God gave me experiment mercy, so that in my thirty years as an instructor in the chemistry laboratory no student got hurt under my supervision. In February 1955, Miss Carolyn Huntley, who is one of the best students at Huntington College, had an explosion in an experiment in the chemistry laboratory; a bottle exploded with flying pieces of glass and acid. It frightened an Indian student who was ten feet away, but no one got hurt. I feel that in all walks of life we should pray for guidance and protection, for we are living in a dangerous world. We need the Lord's protection physically, mentally, and spiritually.

In Lingnan University one student nearly added concentrated sulfuric acid to a bottle containing potassium chlorate to produce a serious explosion which could have injured his eyes very badly had I not stopped him at the right moment. He was mistaking potassium chlorate for potassium chloride, as he was short-sighted.

When I visited my daughter in California in April, 1956 I was fixing a motion picture projector. A small screw dropped on the floor. We tried to find it many times, using a vacuum cleaner, as I was afraid that my one-year-old granddaughter, Doris, might pick it up and swallow it. God answered my prayers, for I saw Doris pick it up the next morning and put it into her mouth. I was thrilled and told her to spit it out. There have been many incidents like this in our experiences at home. This shows that the Lord is with us wherever we go and He watches over us and is ready to help us whenever we are conscious of His presence and bring our problems to Him.